Tales of the Wicklow Hills

2000 Years of History, Myth, Legend and Local Stories

Richard Marsh

Foreword by Dáithí Ó hÓgáin

Department of Irish Folklore, University College Dublin

Legendary Books Series, Volume 1
Tales of the Wicklow Hills: 2000 Years of History, Myth, Legend and Local Stories
ISBN 978-0-9557568-0-1

Published by

Richard Marsh
15 Fontenoy Street
Dublin 7, Ireland
Phone +353-1-8827941

www.legendarytours.com
email richardmarsh@legendarytours.com

Also by Richard Marsh:
The Legends and Lands of Ireland, Sterling, New York, 2004; pbk 2006

I would like to express my appreciation to the staffs at the National Library of Ireland, the library of the Royal Society of Antiquaries of Ireland (especially Siobhán de hÓir), the Irish Traditional Music Archive, the Department of Irish Folklore library at University College Dublin, and Dr Dáithí Ó hÓgáin of the same Department for his invaluable advice. I also wish to thank the Folklore of Ireland Society for permission to use extracts from Pádraig Ó Tuathail's interview with Mrs O'Toole in the chapter on Michael Dwyer.

A version of "Hempenstall – the Walking Gallows", part of "Michael Dwyer", and parts of "The Vale of Avoca" were broadcast on RTÉ Radio One.

Title page engraving of Glendalough by F. G. Bruce, from *The Dublin Penny Journal*, November 8, 1834.

Front cover: The Gates of Heaven, Kilranelagh Cemetery. See page 69.

Back cover: 1798 Wicklow Freedom Fighters Stone, Glenmalure. Note the names of Michael Dwyer and Sam McAllister. See Michael Dwyer chapter.

All photos by the author.

Contents

Map Showing Places Mentioned in the Text
by Christine Warner

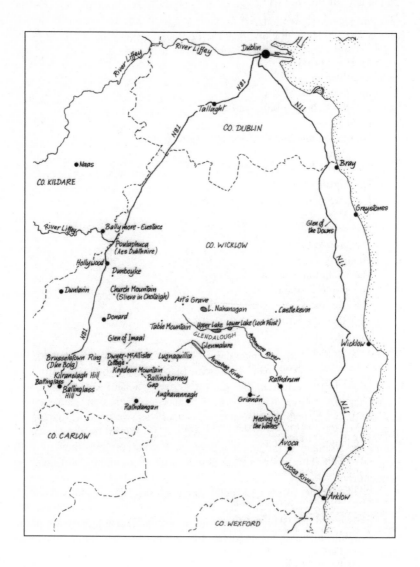

Foreword

Storytelling is one of the principal means of humanising our environment, for in it one encounters the rationalisation and imagination, the great human heart of the world. It is therefore essential to our modern communities that people have at their disposal all the resources which cultivate and develop this practice, the heritage lore and the speaking voice of tradition, continuing and constantly interpreted.

I know of few other people in this context with the knowledge, the ability, the initiative, and the skills of communication of Richard Marsh. Scholar and poet, he is a man of great conviviality and collegiality in the pursuit of knowledge and of all the cultural data which evoke our interest and accordingly make our life more interesting. His open-minded attitude, constant pursuit of sources, and his aesthetic taste are a fine example to follow. Every part of Ireland should have its Richard Marsh, and Wicklow is particularly lucky in this regard. He shows us that the heritage of storytelling is expressed in both literary and oral forms, making the landscape and the life of the various communities more colourful in the mind, more adventurous and fulfilling. As such it is of importance to the young as well as to the old, for a Wicklow person should be more interesting and entertaining, more socially expressive, if he or she can represent to the rest of Ireland and to the world a particular sense and a special atmosphere of Wicklow.

The selection of stories and traditions here is far-reaching and inclusive – from local heroes, saints, and other worthies of the dim and distant past to some figures whose silhouettes stand out more clearly in the light of history. Here we can read of striking and dramatic individuals. There are the mythical Eithne, legendary Cormac and fictional Buchet, the historical Kevin and Rónán, the great Fiacha mac Aodha Ó Broin of Elizabethan times, down to the patriot heroes Michael Dwyer and Sam McAllister of the Great Rising of 1798. There are many others too, heroes and freedom-fighters, rogues and renegades, as well as a myriad of characters who all in their own way have left an imprint on the canvas of history and an image in the prism of heritage. Richard presents them all with great verve and skill, and in such a homely light as to allow them linger in the memory.

Fearaim fáilte roimh an leabhar suntasach seo, agus is mór an sásamh dom é a sheoladh go sábháilte sítheoilte ar chonairí casta an tseanchais. Nár laga Dia an lámh a scríobh, agus nár ídí an peann. Treise le Risteard, an té atá ag oscailt fuinneog na hoidhreachta dúinn agus ag ligint an tsolais isteach!

Dáithí Ó hÓgáin
Dr Ó hÓgáin is the author of *The Lore of Ireland: An Encyclopaedia of Myth, Legend and Romance*, The Collins Press, 2006.

Preface

These stories of fact and fancy range from the 1st century BC "Naming of Baltinglass", part of the mythological history of Ireland, to current oral accounts of recent incidents in "The Vale of Avoca". Some stories, such as those of Feagh McHugh O'Byrne, Michael Dwyer, and John Moore, are well documented in reliable sources of history, if sometimes highly coloured in re-tellings. Many are legends based on historical personages or events, for example "Hempenstall" and Saint Kevin. Some are at least partially myth, such as "The Melodies of Buchet's House" with the fertility god figure of Buchet ("hundred cows"). "Fingal Rónáin" is literary historical fiction. Where the distinction is not obvious, I have provided guidance in the text or notes.

The Avoca stories are a microcosm of local tradition, ranging from international migratory folklore attached to the Mottee Stone, to the factual incidents of the moving statue and the historical basis of The Big Snow. In between are brief tales told to me by people who believed they were true, and of course the mystery of the Tigroney ghost that I provisionally solved.

The footnotes give sources and additional facts not essential to the appreciation of the stories as such. Background material is provided in introductions to the chapters and the Notes at the end of the text.

Translations are mine, except where otherwise noted.

Richard Marsh

Come all ye gallant Irishmen
And listen unto me.
I'll sing for you a verse or two
That's mixed with history.
I am a true-born Wicklowman,
And the same I'll ne'er deny,
And my dwelling is surrounded by
The Wicklow Mountains high.
first stanza of "The Wicklow Mountains High" (traditional)

"Other nationalities may laugh when we describe our modest land elevations as mountains. But they're ours, they're the biggest we've got, we're proud of them, and we'll call them what we like." – Mattie Lennon, from the film *Sunrise on the Wicklow Hills*, West Wicklow Films, 2005

The Naming of Baltinglass

Before 19th- and early 20th-century translators unlocked the treasures of Irish manuscripts, place-name theories were limited only by the imaginations of antiquaries, the amateur proto-archaeologists of the 19th century. In the case of Baltinglass:

> ... *Baal-Tin-Glas*, signifying, according to common acceptation, "the pure fire of Baal," and is thence supposed to have been one of the principal seats of druidical worship.[1]

> ... *Beal-tinne-glas* or *the fire of Beal's mysteries*, the fires being lighted there by the Druids in honour of the sun.[2]

> ... *Bal-teach-glas*, or *the town of the grey houses* [3]

Uaim-Belaigh Conglais, the "Cave of the pass of Cuglais." In Medieval documents the name was modified to Balkynglas, and now corruptly Baltinglass, about which modern Fire-worshippers have written a great deal of nonsense.[4]

All modern experts agree that the name derives from *Belach Con Glais* (The Road of the Hound of Glas): "*belach dubhtaire*, which to-day men call *belach Conglaise* or 'Baltinglass'".[5] The prose *Rennes Dindshenchas* (Lore of Place-names) tells the story behind the derivation. Characters and the reaving event – part of the story The Destruction of Dá Derga's Hostel – place the incident in the 1st century BC.

> Glas was seventh son of Donn Desa and a fosterling of Etirscel the Great, King of Ireland. In Tara Glas was reared and 'tis he that was Master of the Hounds both with Etirscel and Conaire. Now when his (six) brothers went a-reaving to Ingcél, Glas proceeded with his hounds into the plain of Tara, and there he met with a wild pig which went away before him southwards as far as yon Pass, and there fell the pig and the hounds and Glas (himself), whence Belach Conglais.[6]

---

[1] Lewis, op. cit.

[2] Joyce, *Origin and History*, quoting from "Seward's Topographical Dictionary".

[3] Ibid., quoting from "the writer of a Guide to Wicklow (Curry, Dublin, 1834)".

[4] Shearman, p. 14n. *Uath* (Shearman's "Uaim") can mean "cave", but in this case it is probably a variant of *urtha* ("[here] begins") at the beginning of the title of a medieval version of the tale. There is no cave in the story, though there is one on Baltinglass Hill.

[5] O'Grady, *Silva Gadelica*, ii, p. 408.

[6] Stokes, "Rennes Dindshenchas", p. 421.

That short tale is one of two incidents set in the Baltinglass area which are part of a longer story, The Swine of Drebrenn. Drebrenn was a sister of Queen Maeve of Connacht and daughter of Eochaidh Feidlach, 1st-century BC King of Ireland. She was also the lover of Aonghus son of the Dagda. She had three foster sisters who were married to three brothers. The girls' mother, Garbhdalbh ("Coarse-face") did not approve of the matches, and one day when the three couples were gathering nuts in the woods near Tara, she transformed them into demon pigs.

Their names in pig form were Crainchrin, Coelcheis and Treilech for the women and Fraechan, Banban and Brogarban for the men. Like the Children of Lir, who were transformed into swans, the pigs retained their human reason and speech. They went to Buchet, who was a guesthouse-keeper at Kilranelagh Hill near Baltinglass famed for his hospitality.[7] After a year, Buchet's wife "was seized with longing for a steak off Brogarban's belly". From the *Metrical Dindshenchas*:

> It was a grief to Brogarban of Brega
> when the woman's husband told him of it:
> "Let us slay the white woman,"
> said Buichet to Brogarban.

> "No evil hath thy wife deserved of me,"
> said then the white-flanked swine:
> "if she desire a steak of my tender flesh,
> she shall have it for thy sake, brave warrior!"

> She mustered – foolish was the woman –
> a hundred warriors, a hundred dogs followed them,
> a hundred spears, a hundred shields sharp-edged,
> it was for the killing of Brogarban.

> Brogarban of Borg Brain destroyed them
> by his unaided prowess,
> and he spared the woman
> for the sake of Buichet, whose wife she was.[8]

Brogarban then led the other Swine to Brú na Bóinne (Newgrange), where they stayed under the protection of Aonghus, and then they were with Drebrenn at Glascarn (possibly near Mullingar) for a year. According to the story of the naming of Mag Mucrame (The Plain of Pig-counting) in County Galway, they broke out of the Cave of Cruachan, an Otherworld portal from which monsters in various forms regularly issued, to embark on a seven-year

---

[7] See The Melodies of Buchet's House chapter.
[8] Gwynn, *Metrical Dindshenchas* III, pp. 389-91.

rampage that laid waste to Ireland: wherever they went, nothing would grow again behind them. Glas's chase of the pig is set in this period.

The Swine could not be caught or killed. If a spear was thrown or a sword swung at them, they disappeared. No one could accurately count them until one day Queen Maeve and her consort Aillil came to the plain thenceforth known as Mag Mucrame –

> to hunt them and number them aright:
> and they were found upon the bright sands
> in their lairs in Mag Fráich.
>
> The hunters set to chase them one by one,
> and to count them right heedfully;
> to Medb at Belach na Fert
> they were brought all together at a marsh.
>
> One pig, deer-like in hue, made a spring,
> and Medb caught hold of his strong foot,
> and with the haste of danger he left
> his skin in one of her hands.[9]

This broke the pigs' magic power, making it possible to count them. Five were pursued to various parts of the country and killed where place-names commemorate them. And so "they all fell save Brogarban, and their five heads were brought to that mound. Whence *Dumae Selga* [The Mound of the Hunt]." [10]

What became of Brogarban if he was not killed is nowhere mentioned, but alternatively:

> … Glascharn:
> the six trenches thou seest on the hill,
> they are the beds of the warrior-swine.[11]

---

[9] Gwynn, *Metrical Dindshenchas* III, p. 385.

[10] Stokes, "The Rennes Dindshenchas", p. 472. Duma Selga is east of the inauguration mound of Carnfree, about three miles south of Rathcroghan near Tulsk in County Roscommon.

[11] Gwynn, *Metrical Dindshenchas* III, p. 391.

The Melodies of Buchet's House

There was a "cauldron of hospitality" among the Leinstermen named Buchet. Buchet's House was a guesthouse or *bruiden* for the warriors of Ireland, located at Kilranelagh Hill near Baltinglass. The fire beneath Buchet's cooking pot had never been extinguished since he became a hospitaller, and he was renowned for his generosity.

Cathaoir Mór was the last Leinster king to be king of Ireland. He had twelve sons and a daughter named Eithne Tabhfhada ("of the Long Side", ie, Slender). Eithne was the most beautiful woman of her time, and if a young man told his girlfriend that she was as beautiful as Eithne, it would be taken as a great compliment.

She was the foster daughter of Buchet and his wife. Eithne's brothers loved their sister so much that they used to visit her at Buchet's House, not just once in a while, but quite frequently. And they stayed not only for a weekend or so, but for weeks at a time. Because they were sons of the king of Ireland, they had large retinues of friends and servants, and these also came with them to Buchet's House.

After some years of this, Buchet, who had been a wealthy man with seven herds of cattle, was reduced to only one herd of seven cows and a bull. He went to see Cathaoir Mór at Tara.

"My wife and I are happy to have Eithne as our foster daughter, and we are delighted that her brothers come to visit her. But could you please ask them not to come so often and not to stay so long and not to bring so many people? Their visits have made me a poor man."

Cathaoir Mór, who had held the kingship of Ireland for nearly thirty years, said, "I am an old man now with no strength. I can no longer run or jump or tell my sons how to live their lives. If you are a poor man, all I can do is recommend that you move to a smaller house."

So Buchet and his wife and Eithne moved to a small cottage in Kells, County Meath, with an earthen floor covered by rushes. Soon after that, Cathaoir Mór died, and Maeve of the Red Side, king-maker and sovereignty goddess of Leinster and Tara, decided to take the kingship for herself for a while.

The young Cormac mac Art, who was to become the most famous of the high kings, was living in Kells at this time, waiting until Maeve finished taking her turn at the kingship. He had little to do to pass the time but watch the world go by, and he took a particular interest in that part of the world in which Eithne moved as she went about her household chores. Perhaps being young, Cormac was a bit shy in the face of such beauty as Eithne's, and he broke the ice with a chat-up line more suitable for a teenager than a future king:

"I notice that when you gather the rushes for the floor, you make three bundles, and one bundle of the best rushes is set aside. And when you fetch water, you fill two buckets from the side of the river and one from the middle of the stream, where the water is clearest. And when you milk the cows, you set apart one bucket that contains the most cream. Can you tell me why you do that?"

"I do it to give honour to one who deserves great honour. If I could do more to give him honour I would."

"And who might that be?"

"Buchet the Hospitaller, my foster father."

"Are you Eithne of the Long Side?"

"I am."

"It may be that I can help you give Buchet greater honour."

So when Cormac became king, he married Eithne.[12] Because her father, Cathaoir Mór, was dead, he gave the bride price to her foster father, Buchet. He took Buchet to the ramparts of Kells, which is built on a hill. When a king wanted to give someone a great gift, he often took him to a high place and gave him all he could see. Cormac went one better than that. He gave Buchet all he could see for a week – not only the land, but also all the cows and people and oxen and horses that passed by in that time.

Buchet went back to his House in Wicklow a very wealthy man. But did his new wealth affect his far-famed generosity? Only for the better.

People used to talk about the melodies of Buchet's House. They meant not only the melodies of fifty warriors in their purple clothes and battle harness, playing and singing when the company was intoxicated; the melodies of fifty young women in their purple mantles and long yellow-gold hair streaming over their clothes, dancing and playing among the guests when they were sober; and the melodies of fifty harps soothing the company until morning; but they spoke especially of the melody of Buchet's voice when he greeted each guest with a light laughing smile and these words:

"You are very welcome. There is plenty to eat and drink, and you may regard this house as your own house. You are going to be very happy here, and I am going to be happy because you're happy."

And that is why this story is called "The Melodies of Buchet's House".[13]

---

[12] Their son was Cairbre Liffechair ("Liffey-lover"), so called because he was fostered near the Liffey. High king 268-84, he killed and was killed by Oscar, son of Oisín son of Fionn mac Cumhaill, in the Battle of Gabhra (Garristown, Co. Meath) in 284.

[13] This is a mostly free and partly close translation of the edition in Greene's *Fingal Rónáin*, with interpolations giving the historical context.

Saint Kevin and Glendalough

Glendalough
(Gleann Dá Loch – "Glen of the Two Lakes")

> I do not know if there is any tune about Glendaloch, but if there be, it must be the most delicate, fantastic, fairy melody that ever was played. Only fancy can describe the charms of that delightful place. ... Thomas Moore has written rather an awful description of it ...
>
> *Thackeray,* The Irish Sketch-book*, 1843*

During the Dark Ages, when law and order had broken down on the Continent, the light of learning was kept alive at half a dozen university-monasteries in Ireland, giving the country a lasting reputation as the Land of Saints and Scholars. Glendalough, "the luminary of the Western World, whence savage septs [clans] and roving barbarians derived the benefits of knowledge and the blessings of religion",[14] was founded by Saint Kevin in the 6th century. Books, food and accommodation were provided free of charge. In 1214, the Archbishop of Tuam reported that Glendalough had become a den of thieves and robbers. However, it survived raids by Vikings and "the English adventurers", and flourished until it was destroyed as a city by the English in 1398, in spite of Kevin's curse that anyone who ravaged his church would suffer from tumour, scrofula, anthrax, and madness.

Glendalough continued to be occupied by the native Irish, who found it a haven relatively safe from government oppression and nearly as secure as Glenmalure, though somewhat closer to Dublin. The English sometimes confused the two side-by-side cul-de-sac glens, and some accounts of Feagh McHugh O'Byrne's 1580 massacre of the English troops in Glenmalure place the battle in Glendalough.

In June 1798, a group of captured Orangemen was taken to the 10th-century round tower in the ruins of the monastic city to be executed, but there were objections to the desecration of a holy site. The prisoners were then taken to the cemetery, but similar objections were raised. Finally they were marched up the hill away from sacred ground, but by this time the would-be executioners had tired of the sport, and the Orangemen were spared.

Seven pilgrimages to Glendalough equalled one to Rome, but religious tourism eventually degenerated into large commercial fairs that attracted unsavoury elements and violence, as happened elsewhere in Ireland. Although the Church put an end to mass pilgrimages to Glendalough in 1862, many people still come privately on Kevin's feast day, 3 June.

---

[14] Archdall, p. 775.

For several hundred years after Kevin, Glendalough was the religious administrative centre for a wide area on both sides of the hills. The Wicklow kings were buried at the Reefert (*Rí Ferta* – Royal Cemetery) Church at the western end of the glen, because Kevin had arranged with God that anyone buried there would go straight to heaven.

A story is told in Glendalough – though it may not have happened there – about the time George Bernard Shaw and G. K. Chesterton met in Ireland for a holiday. Chesterton, whose ample bulk contrasted with Shaw's spare frame, said to Shaw, "To look at you, anyone would think there was still a famine in Ireland." To which Shaw replied, "And to look at you, Chesterton, anyone would think you caused it." [15]

Kevin and the Thief, the Bird, the Cow, the Water Monster

Some of the stories about Saint Kevin may contain a touch of the fancy Thackeray referred to, and it is probably for this reason that he is one of the best-known local Irish saints. As a celebrated 19th-century guide, Joe Irwin, put it: "Saint Kavin, you must know, Sir, is counted the greatest of all the saints, bekase he went to school with the prophet Jeremiah." [16] Irwin is probably the guide described by Thackeray: "There is an excellent guide on the spot, who, for a shilling or two, will tell all he knows, and a great deal more, too."

Irwin explained the reason for a hole in a headstone near the cathedral. Kevin asked a known thief named Garadh Duff where he got the mare he was riding with a foal at her foot. Garadh Duff said he had bought her from one of the O'Byrnes.

> "That's a lie, I know by your face, you thief."
>
> "Oh, may I never stir out of this spot," says Garadh, "if what I say is not true."
>
> "Dare you tell me so: now in order to make a liar, and a thief, and a holy show of you to the world's end, I'll fix your foal and mare there in that rock, and the print of their hoofs shall remain for ever, and you yourself must die and go to purgatory."
>
> "Well, if I must die," said the thief, "please me, holy father, in one thing, bury me in your own churchyard, and leave a hole in my tombstone, so that if any stray horse or cow should pass by, I may just push up my arm and make a snap at their leg, if it was nothing else but to remind me of my humour, and that I may keep my temper during the long day of the grave." [17]

---

[15] Vose, p. 24.

[16] Lover, *Legends and Stories*, p. 13.

[17] *Dublin Penny Journal*, Vol. III, No. 123, November 8, 1834, p. 148.

Saint Kevin was 120 years old when he died in the year 618.[18] Raised by Christian parents in Cualu Uí Cheallaigh (where Counties Dublin, Wicklow and Kildare meet), Kevin decided early on that he wanted to be a hermit. He left his parents' home and walked over the Wicklow Hills until he came to Glendalough, which was uninhabited except for a water monster (*péist*) that lived in the Upper Lake. Kevin lived contentedly in the stump of a hollow tree at the closed end of the glen next to the larger of the two lakes in the glen, the Upper Lake, ate the fruits and nuts that grew wild in the glen, and dressed in the skins of animals that had died of old age, because he wouldn't kill an animal.

Kevin disliked people, but he loved animals, and he and the water monster got on well as neighbours. Pictures of Kevin often show him holding a bird in one hand. One day when he was standing up to his waist in the Upper Lake praying with his arms outstretched, a blackbird built a nest in his hand. Kevin remained in that position until the bird had laid her eggs, the eggs had hatched, and the baby birds were able to fly away.

A farmer named Dima was taking his cows on a grazing tour, and when he arrived at Glendalough he noticed that one of his cows gave fifty times her usual output. When he found that she went to Kevin and spent the whole day licking his feet, Dima declared, "That man must be a saint." He brought Kevin home and cleaned him up and spread the word about the miracle of the cow's milk. Pilgrims began to flock to Glendalough to be near the holy man.

This was a mixed blessing. Kevin hated crowds, but the water monster now had home-delivered meals. However, Kevin negotiated a compromise in which the monster moved to the Lower Lake, which is still labelled Loch Péist (Lake of the Monster) on maps and signposts. Farmers washed their animals in the Upper Lake, and the monster ate the dirt and

---

[18] Archdall, p. 766. Some sources differ, but Kevin's 1500th birthday was celebrated in 1998 by a Catholic religious group based in Glendalough.

diseases that flowed into the Lower Lake. Loch Péist appears to be péist-free now, but there is a lake called Loch na hOnchon (also called Lough Nahanagan) on Camaderry on the north side of the glen. It is possible that this is the water monster's new home. *Onchú* means "savage beast".

(Hydraulics engineers from other countries visit Loch na hOnchon to observe the workings of the Turlough Hill pumped water storage scheme. During periods of low electricity demand, water is pumped through an underground pipe 300m uphill from Loch na hOnchon to a reservoir. When demand peaks and extra power is needed, electricity is generated by letting the water flow back into Loch na hOnchon. At least, that's the official explanation, but if the water monster really did move there ...)

Before Kevin's time, Saint Patrick took a tour around Ireland with Oisín, son of Fionn mac Cumhaill, to hear the stories of how places got their names. When they arrived at Glendalough and Oisín told Patrick about Loch Péist, Patrick asked why Fionn hadn't killed the monster, as he had so many others. Oisín said it was because Fionn knew that Kevin would come along in a few centuries to sort out the problem.

Kevin Goes to Hollywood

Kevin became a religious superstar, and from time to time to get away from the crowds he would walk twelve miles west over the hills via the Wicklow Gap to the village now known as Hollywood, where he stayed by himself in a cave called Kevin's Bed (not to be confused with the cave in Glendalough also called Kevin's Bed). Kevin probably discovered this cave when he went to that area to start a new church. That time, he was carried in a litter by servants. When they reached the village then called Cnoc Rua (Red Hill), from the colour of the summer vegetation on the hill south of the village, they found their way blocked by a wood, and they stopped.

"Why did you stop?" said Kevin.

"There are trees in the way," they said.

"Don't worry," Kevin told them. "Just keep walking."

They walked toward the wood, and the trees fell down in front of them to make a road. Kevin blessed the wood and promised "hell and a short life to any one who should burn either green wood or dry from this wood till doom".[19] That is how the village got its name, Holy Wood ("Sanctum Nemus" or "Sanctus Boscus" or "Seinbois" in medieval records), which by the 16th century became Hollywood. (A local man, Matthew Guirke, was responsible for naming Hollywood, California.) It is also called *Cillín Chaoibhín* in Irish, which means "Kevin's Chapel". One local tradition says the church Kevin built was on the site of the church ruins and graveyard at

---

[19] Plummer, p. 123.

Dunboyke, which can be seen looking east from the Athgreany Stone Circle.[20]

If you stand at the entrance of Kevin's Bed (Hollywood) and look down into the valley, you can see the location used for the ambush scene in the film *Michael Collins*. The ambush happened in County Cork, but the topography here perfectly fits the actual site as it was in 1922, with the addition of a road built especially for the film. The white statue at the top of the hill that you see briefly in the ambush scene is Saint Kevin, and just under it is the cave. A hermit who lived in the cave in the 1960s told the children he was Saint Kevin, and they believed him. He left an inscription painted on the wall: "Help me Lord to find my true home." Looking north from the cave, you can see the motte (a man-made defensive hill) on a natural stone outcrop where the "castle of St Nemus", granted to the Anglo-Norman Geoffrey de Marisco in 1192, was located.

Kevin and King O'Toole

The story of how Kevin acquired the extensive lands for his monastery, of which he became abbot in 570, is told in the words of the above-mentioned guide, Joe Irwin, in the enduring literary folk tale "King O'Toole and St Kevin" by Samuel Lover. King O'Toole, owner of Glendalough and surrounding territory, was kept entertained in his old age by a pet goose.

> You see, the goose used for to swim acrass the lake, and go down divin' for throut, (and not finer throut in all Ireland, than the same throut), and cotch fish on a Friday for the king, and flew every other day round about the lake, divartin' the poor king, that you'd think he'd break his sides laughin' at the frolicksome tricks av his goose; so in coorse o' time the goose was the greatest pet in the counthry; and the biggest rogue, and divarted the king to no end, and the poor king was as happy as the day was long.[21]

In the course of time, the goose herself was stricken in years and King O'Toole was "done out of all divarshin". Kevin offered to restore the goose to her prime in exchange for all the ground she flew over after the cure. The king agreed, and Kevin blessed the goose and threw her into the air. In short, she flew all around the valley, but in Lover's story the guide recites the tale

---

[20] In 1220, Henry, Archbishop of Dublin, granted to the prioress and nuns of the nunnery at Timolin this "church of St. Keivin of Dunboc with its appurtenances". (Archdall, p. 343)

[21] Lover, *Legends and Stories*, where the story is prefaced with the first four lines of Thomas Moore's "By that Lake, Whose Gloomy Shore".

attached to every landmark she passes over, including the Poulanass waterfall, which a Miss Rafferty had a year earlier fallen into and was rescued from by a young Dublin man ("he was out o' Francis-street, I hear") whom she then married. The story is continued in a 19th-century ballad that has passed into folk tradition.

King O'Toole and St. Kevin[22]
(From the Legend of Samuel Lover)
By J. Kearney
Air: "Down in Our Village" / "Pretty Little Dear"

Saint Kevin once was travelling through a place called Glendalough,
He chanced to meet with King O'Toole, and axed him for a shough;[23]
Says the king, "you're but a stranger, for your face I've never seen,
But if you have e'en a taste o' a weed I'll lend you my dhudheen." [24]

While the saint was kindling up his pipe, the monarch gave a sigh.
"Is there anything the matter," says the saint, "that makes you cry?"
Says the king, "I had a gander that was left me by my mother,
And this morning he has cocked his toes with some disease or other."

"And are you crying for the gander, you unfortunate old goose!
Dry up your tears, in fretting sure the devil take the use."
Says the saint, "What would you give me if your gander I'd revive?"
Says the king, "I'll be your sarvint all the days that I'm alive."

"I'll cure him," says St. Kevin, "but I want no sarvint-man;
But if I'd not make too bould to ax, I'd like a bit o' land;
As you think so much about the bird, if I make him whole and sound,
Will you give me the taste of land the gander does fly round?"

"In troth I will, in welcome," says the king, "give what you ask;"
The saint bid him bring the gander, and he would begin the task;
The king went to the palace to fetch him out the bird,
Though he had not the least intention of sticking to his word.

Saint Kevin took the gander from the arms of the king,
He first began to twig his beak, and then to stretch his wing;

---

[22] *Harding's Dublin Songster*, Vol. 2, No. 15 (c.1850), p. 350. The version that the late Micho Russell had from his mother is in his book (Russell, pp. 32-4) and is sung by him on the 1975 cassette *The Russell Family of Doolin, Co. Clare* (Celtic Music KTSC 251). Another version can be heard on *The Maid of Eirin* by Grianán (WW CD 004), 1993.

[23] Puff on a pipe. Rhymes with "Glendalough".

[24] Pipe.

He hooshed him up into the air – he flew thirty miles around;
Says the saint, "I'd thank your majesty for that little bit o' ground."

The king, to raise a ruction, faith he called the saint a witch,
And sent in for his six big sons to heave him in a ditch;
"Nabocklish," [25] says Saint Kevin, "Now I'll settle these young urchins" –
He turned the king and his six sons into the Seven Churches!

Thus King O'Toole had suffered for his dishonest doings;
The saint then left the gander there to guard about the ruins:
If you go there on a summer day, between twelve and one o'clock,
You'll see the gander flying round the glen of Glendalough.

Now I think there is a moral good attached unto this song.
To punish men I think is right whenever they do wrong;
A poor man may keep his word much better than the folk that's grander,
For the king begrudged to pay the saint when he cured his ould dead gander.

Kevin and Fáelán

A local king, Colmán Mór son of Coirpre, divorced his wife, Dassan, and married a younger woman, Fedelm. Dassan was a witch, and she used her magic arts to kill the first two children Colmán had by Fedelm. When their third child, a boy named Fáelán, was born, Colmán sent him to live with Kevin as his foster son to protect him from Dassan. One day, Dassan appeared on the top of Derrybawn, the hill that forms the south side of Glendalough, and directed magic spells against Kevin and Fáelán down below. Kevin countered with his power from God, and they fought a duel. Dassan moved around the rim of the glen until she was on Camaderry on the north side of the glen. Kevin aimed a bolt of power that killed her, and she tumbled down the far side of Camaderry into the next glen to the north, which is now called Glendassan.

One time there was a shortage of milk in Glendalough, and Kevin was worried that Fáelán wouldn't have enough. Berach, an itinerant saint to whom the killing of Dassan is often attributed, was staying in Glendalough at the time.

[Berach] sained [blessed] the mountain and said: "Let the doe with her fawn that is on the mountain come hither." And the doe came at

---

[25] Ná bac leis - "You're welcome" (lit. "Don't bother with it.")

once with her fawn following her; and she was milked every day for Fáelán. One day, however, there came a wolf, and killed the doe's fawn and ate it; and the doe did not give her milk without the fawn. Kevin was troubled at this. So Berach sained the mountain, and said: "Let the animal who did the disservice, do service." Thereupon the wolf came and settled himself on his paws before the doe; and the doe licked the wolf, and gave her milk at the sight of him. And the wolf would come at every milking time; and the doe would be milked in his presence.[26]

The doe left the milk she produced in a bowl-like hollow in a bullán stone that you can see just across the bridge from the little church known as "Kevin's Kitchen". The bridge is called Droichet na h-Eillte – Bridge of the Doe. (Glendalough used to be known as "the bullán capital of Ireland" for the large number of bullán stones found there, but most of them have mysteriously disappeared in recent years.)

Fáelán (d. 666) became king of Leinster, and from two of his descendants, Leinster kings Bran (d. 838) and Tuathal (d. 854) through Bran Mut of the Bórama saga, are descended the O'Byrnes and O'Tooles of Wicklow. Fáelán's brother or half-brother, Rónán mac Colmáin (d. 624), is one of the historical kings on whom the story "Fingal Rónáin" is partially based.

Kevin and Cathleen

When Kevin was staying in Glendalough, he lived in the small partially man-made cave, believed to have been a Bronze Age burial chamber, called Kevin's Bed (not to be confused with the Kevin's Bed in Hollywood) in the face of a cliff eight metres (25 feet) above the Upper Lake. This cave was later frequented as a place of retreat by the 12th-century archbishop of Dublin, Saint Laurence O'Toole, and it served Michael Dwyer as a hideout. A young woman named Cathleen had a crush on Kevin, and she used to annoy him by asking him if she could clean his cave, cook his dinner, warm his bed for him. Now, if there was anything Kevin hated worse than people in general, it was women in particular, because according to Kevin's theory a man can't become a saint if he has anything to do with women.

Although he stripped naked and rolled in a bed of nettles in front of Cathleen, and then beat her with a bunch of nettles to cool her ardour, Kevin found her one day in his cave. He lost his patience and pushed her out of the cave, and she fell into the lake and drowned. But he was very kind to animals.

---

[26] Plummer, p. 28.

Since that day, the sun never shines on the Upper Lake, and birds never sing there. The local tradition that Kevin prayed – with an implied guarantee – that no one would drown thereafter in the lake is contradicted by a vaguely worded 1834 article in the *Dublin Penny Journal*. A distraught young pregnant woman and her sister tumbled from the ledge called "Lady's Leap" just above Kevin's Bed and were drowned.

A 19th-century travel writer accused local tour guides of inventing the Cathleen story for their own profit. However, three leading 19th-century literary figures, Gerald Griffin (1803-40), Thomas Moore (1779-1852), and Samuel Lover (1797-1868) and at least one Anon have celebrated this one-sided romance in verse. Griffin's version ("it contains some exquisite passages, all fraught with chasteness of expression and beauty of thought")[27] begins in Luggala and rambles on for 56 earnest and now forgotten stanzas. Here is a summary with excerpts.

The Fate of Cathleen

Young Kevin and young Cathleen, a lord's daughter ("I've left for thee my natal hall"), stand by the lake "in Luggelaw's deep-wooded vale", and she confesses her love for him. Kevin rejects her:

> "Oh, wouldst thou bribe my heart to sin ...?
> And what to thee seems pure from ill
> To me looks dark with danger."

Cathleen agrees to leave him alone and go home, only to discover:

> "But now the even is falling late,
> The way is long and lonely –
> Oh, let me rest within thy gate
> Till morning rises only!"

Well, after all, Kevin rationalises to himself, "Those who take the stranger in / Have patriarchal merit," so they spend the night in Kevin's modest accommodation in separate "bowers". In the morning, after a night of troubled dreams, Kevin wakes up first, peeps in at the sleeping Cathleen, and – "For, oh, the blood within his veins / Was warm, and young, and human" – he bends over her to plant a kiss on her lips. But before he makes contact, two things happen simultaneously: she murmurs "My Kevin!" in her dreams, and the nearby church bell tolls for a funeral.

---

[27] *Irish Literary Gazette*, 27 March 1858, p. 196.

Kevin takes the divine hint and flees across "each mimic Alp" of the hills all the way to Bray. Cathleen, who had a late start, follows his footprints in the dew "for in her breast / Deep passion fierce was burning".

> Night fell – day rose – night fell again,
> And the dim day-dawn found her ...

... succeeding in tracking Kevin to the Bed above the Upper Lake in Glendalough, where he is asleep and having a nightmare in which she has barred the gates of Heaven against him. Bending over him, she is just about to kiss him, when he wakes up from the nightmare, sees her, and nearly kills her in his confusion. He warns her:

> "Fly far, and hate and fear me;
> For death is on this gloomy shore,
> And madness haunting near me."

"Never," says Cathleen, abandoning the remnants of her shyness and flinging her arms around him. Kevin pushes her into the lake and she is drowned. Griffin, who joined the Christian Brothers shortly before his death, managed to put a positive spin on the grim ending:

> Oh, tempted at that saintly height,
> If they to earth sank lowly,
> She ne'er had been an angel bright,
> Nor he a victor holy!

And with a nod towards the local tradition about birds not singing over the lake:

> The lark ne'er wakes the ruddy morn
> Above that gloomy water.

Moore installed his tongue firmly in his cheek and disposed of the tragic story in a mere forty lines (in the fourth number of *Irish Melodies* in 1811), of which the first two are still well known and frequently quoted.

By That Lake, Whose Gloomy Shore
(air: "The Brown Irish Girl")

> By that lake, whose gloomy shore
> Skylark never warbles o'er,
> Where the cliff hangs high and steep

Young Saint Kevin stole to sleep.
"Here, at least," he calmly said,
"Woman ne'er shall find my bed."
Ah! the good Saint little knew
What that wily sex can do.

*   *   *

Ah, your Saints have cruel hearts!
Sternly from his bed he starts,
And with rude, repulsive shock,
Hurls her from the beetling rock.

Glendalough! thy gloomy wave
Soon was gentle Kathleen's grave;
Soon the saint (yet, ah! too late)
Felt her love, and mourn'd her fate.
When he said, "Heav'n rest her soul!"
Round the lake light music stole;
And her ghost was seen to glide,
Smiling, o'er the fatal tide!

Lover was considerably more worldly than Griffin. In *Legends and Stories of Ireland*, he described one character as: "a great favourite with the women; he had a smile and a wink for the craythurs at every hand's turn, and the soft word, and the _____ . The short and the long of it is, he was the *divil* among the girls." [28] For all the "exquisite passages" of Griffin and "beautiful little melody" of Moore, it is the irreverent version in Lover's 1839 *Songs and Ballads* that survives today through its offspring.

St. Kevin: A Legend of Glendalough
by Samuel Lover

At Glendalough lived a young saint,
In odor of sanctity dwelling,
An old-fashion'd odor, which now
We seldom or never are smelling;
A book or a hook were to him
The utmost extent of his wishes;
Now, a snatch at the "lives of the saints;"
Then, a catch at the lives of the fishes.

---

[28] Lover, *Legends and Stories*, p. 82.

There was a young woman one day,
Stravagin along by the lake, sir;
She looked hard at St. Kevin, they say,
But St. Kevin no notice did take, sir.
When she found looking hard wouldn't do,
She look'd soft – in the old sheep's eye fashion;
But, with all her sheep's eyes, she could not
In St. Kevin see signs of soft passion.

"You're a great hand at fishing," says Kate;
"'Tis yourself that knows how, faith, to hook them;
But, when you have caught them, agra,
Don't you want a young woman to cook them?"
Says the saint, "I am 'sayrious inclined,'
I intend taking orders for life, dear."
"Only marry," says Kate, "and you'll find
You'll get orders enough from your wife, dear."

"You shall never be flesh of my flesh,"
Says the saint, with an anchorite groan, sir;
"I see that myself," answer'd Kate,
"I can only be 'bone of your bone,' sir.
And even your bones are so scarce,"
Said Miss Kate, at her answers so glib, sir;
"That I think you would not be the worse
Of a little additional rib, sir."

The saint in a rage, seized the lass,
He gave her one twirl round his head, sir,
And, before Doctor Arnott's invention,[29]
Flung her on a watery bed, sir.
Oh! – cruel St. Kevin! – for shame!
When a lady her heart came to barter,
You should not have been Knight of the Bath
But have bowed to the order of Garter.

---

[29] Neil Arnott (1788-1874), M.D., F. R. S., etc., Physician Extraordinary to the Queen, musician, linguist and prolific inventor, devised the "hydrostatic (floating) bed" in 1832 to prevent the serious consequences of bedsores in convalescents. He explains the invention at length in his *Elements of Physics*.

Fingal Rónáin – (The Kin-Slaying of Rónán)
(or The Tragic Death of Mael Fhothartaig)[30]

Rónán mac Aed was a famous king of Leinster in the 7th century. His royal seat was Ráth Imáil near the Glen of Imaal near Baltinglass. Eithne of Munster was his wife, and they had one son, Mael Fhothartaig.

Mael Fhothartaig was always first in the hunt and first in the line of battle, and warriors and kings and their sons used to rise whenever he appeared at their gatherings, so much did they honour him. Because of his great charm and beauty, he was the desire of their daughters and the darling of their women. Mael Fhothartaig had two hounds named Doílín and Dathlenn, who were the best hunting dogs in Ireland at that time, and these hounds were the delight of his life.

Eithne died, and Rónán was without a wife for several years. One day, Mael Fhothartaig said to his father, "Why don't you take a wife? It's not right that you should be alone."

"I have been thinking of that," said Rónán. "I hear that Eochaid Iarlaithe has a lovely daughter ready for marriage."

Eochaid, the last of the Pictish kings in Ireland, was the king of Dál Araidhe in the northeast. The ruins of a successor to his castle, Dunseverick, can still be seen on the north coast of County Antrim near Ballycastle.

"But Father," Mael Fhothartaig said, "surely you're not going to marry such a young lass? Would you not agree with me that a mature, settled woman would be more suitable for you than a skittish girl?"

But if youth fails to heed the wise counsel of age, so age ignores the good advice of youth. Rónán went to Dunseverick and slept with Eochaid's daughter, and he brought her home to Ráth Imáil as his queen. Meanwhile, Mael Fhothartaig, scenting trouble, had gone on a visit into South Leinster.

"Where is your son, Rónán?" said the young queen. "I hear you have a fine son."

"I have, indeed," said Rónán. "He's the best son in Leinster."

"Send for him, then, so he can welcome me and meet my people and see my treasures and jewels."

"I'll send for him, so," said Rónán.

Mael Fhothartaig arrived and gave her a warm welcome.

"You have all our love," he told her. "All our jewels and treasures are yours – for the love you give to Rónán," he emphasised carefully.

"I am so happy to know that you care for me," she said, pointedly using the singular "you".

Rónán's young queen had a beautiful serving maid, and she sent her to tell Mael Fhothartaig that he would be welcome into her – the queen's – bed. Mael Fhothartaig's foster brothers, Congal and Dond, were always with

---

[30] See Notes: Fingal Rónáin for background.

him. One day when they were playing fidchell (a board game like chess), the maid came and joined them. She started to speak, then hesitated and began blushing. The men noticed. Mael Fhothartaig got up and left the room.

"What's wrong with you?" Congal said to the girl.

"The queen wants me to invite Mael Fhothartaig to her bed," said the maid.

"Don't tell Mael Fhothartaig," Congal said. "He'd kill you."

The maid reported this to the queen, who told her to sleep with Mael Fhothartaig and gain his confidence, then give him the message. The maid slept with Mael Fhothartaig, but she was afraid to tell him what the queen wanted. The queen accused her of keeping Mael Fhothartaig for herself and threatened to cut off her head unless she spoke to him. The maid went to Mael Fhothartaig in tears and told him of his stepmother's desire for him.

"I would rather be burnt to ashes than go to her," Mael Fhothartaig said, and he left for Scotland to serve under the king with his hounds Doílín and Dathlenn.

"Every host that was routed before the king of Scotland, and every fight that was won, it was the doing of Mael Fhothartaig." [Kuno Meyer's translation]

Rónán's people demanded that he call Mael Fhothartaig to return. Mael Fhothartaig landed at Dunseverick on his return to Ireland and visited Eochaid.

"Have you slept with my daughter yet?" Eochaid asked him.

"No," Mael Fhothartaig said.

"That is bad," said Eochaid. "I gave her for you, not that old churl."

"That is bad indeed," said Mael Fhothartaig.

Mael Fhothartaig returned to Ráth Imáil, the maid returned to his bed, and the queen resumed her attempted seduction. Mael Fhothartaig turned to his foster brother Congal for advice. Congal offered to cure the queen of her passion if he got a reward. Mael Fhothartaig said he would give him his horse and bridle, but Congal asked for the two hounds, Doílín and Dathlenn. Mael Fhothartaig consented.

Mael Fhothartaig went out to Bae Aife hunting, and Congal sent a message to the queen that he had arranged a tryst for her with Mael Fhothartaig at Bae Aife.

Bae Aife means "the cows of the slope" or "the cows of [the goddess] Aife". They are a group of white quartz boulders lying on the north slope of Kilranelagh Hill, about fifteen minutes' walk from Ráth Imáil. They look like a small herd of cows from a distance.

Congal intercepted the queen on her way to Bae Aife and said, "Where are you going alone, you harlot? You will bring shame on the king." He escorted her home. Then he saw her going to Bae Aife again.

"If I see you again I'll take your head and put it on a stake before the face of Rónán," he said, and this time he drove her home with a horsewhip.

"I'll bring blood to your lips for this," she said.

That night, Mael Fhothartaig's companions returned from the hunt, but Mael Fhothartaig remained outside to avoid the queen. Rónán wondered aloud where Mael Fhothartaig was.

The queen complained, "You're making us deaf always talking about your son."

"It is right for me to speak of him. There has never been a son more faithful to his father. He is a great comfort to me."

"He does not get the comfort from me that he desires," said the queen. "Three times today Congal took me to him at Bae Aife, and your wanton son raped me."

Then she turned to him and showed him her torn head scarf and scratched and bleeding face, which she had torn and scratched herself.

"A curse on your lips, you wicked woman," said Rónán. "That's a lie."

"I'll prove that I speak the truth," said the queen.

At last Mael Fhothartaig came in. It was a cold night. He sat in front of the fire with his back to his father and stepmother warming his shins.

"Verse-capping" was a form of entertainment in those times, indulged in by professional poets and amateurs alike, which continues among Irish speakers today. One person makes up the first two lines of a quatrain and the other finishes it. The queen and Mael Fhothartaig used to do this when they were still on cordial terms, before Mael Fhothartaig learned of her desire for him. The queen recited a half-quatrain that he had capped before:

> "It's cold in the biting wind
> For one who herds Bae Aife."

Mael Fhothartaig answered with the second half of the quatrain, just as the queen expected:

> "It's a useless herding –
> No cows or love to meet you."

To the innocent Mael Fhothartaig, this was merely polite friendliness, but to the ears of Rónán, prepared by his young queen's accusations and inflamed by his own fierce defence of his son's loyalty, it sounded exactly the way the queen wanted it to sound – like a cold and cynical comment about the alleged rape.

"So it's true," said Rónán. Rónán's champion, Aedán, stood nearby.

"Aedán," said Rónán, "a spear into Mael Fhothartaig and another into Congal."

Aedán sent a spear into the back of Mael Fhothartaig's chair where he sat at the fire, and it came out through his breast, pinning him to the chair. Congal leapt up, and Aedán pierced him through the heart with another spear. Rónán's jester, Mac Glas, tried to run away, but Aedán sent a third spear after him. It went through him and spilled out his bowels.

"You've played enough with the men now, Aedán," said Mael Fhothartaig.

Rónán said, "It was bad luck for all of you that you could find no woman to proposition but my wife."

"It was a wretched lie that made you kill your only son, Rónán," Mael Fhothartaig said. "I would sooner sleep with my own mother than with your wife." His last words were: "And Congal didn't deserve to die."

Rónán took Mael Fhothartaig's body into another house and sat next to it for three days, lamenting the loss of his son: "Woe is me, Mael Fhothartaig is slain for the guilt of a lustful woman." [Meyer]

And not forgetting Mael Fhothartaig's hounds, Dathlenn, starving herself in grief, and Doílín, searching in vain for her master:

> "Sad to me is the torture of Dathlenn,
> With rods of steel over her sides
> Our reproach is not on her,
> It is not she who sold our dear ones.

> "[And look at poor] Doílín,
> Thrusting her head into the lap of one after another,
> Seeking one whom she will not find." [Meyer]

Meanwhile, Congal's brother, Dond, took twenty men to the North and sent a message to Eochaid Iarlaithe that his daughter and Mael Fhothartaig had run off together and were coming to see him. Eochaid and his wife and young son went to the border of his territory to greet the supposed runaways, and Dond and his men killed them and cut off their heads. They came back to Ráth Imáil and woke up the young queen by throwing the heads onto her bed. She leapt out of bed and put her knife into her breast and fell on it, so that it came out her back.

Rónán finished his lament and collapsed. Dond then went after Aedán and killed him. This was reported to Rónán, who said, "Dond deserves a reward for his valour and prowess."

Then Rónán said, "I hear battle raging all around the ráth, and I fear this is one battle I am not going to win."

It is not clear whether the Leinstermen revolted when they learned that Rónán had killed Mael Fhothartaig, and there really was a battle, or if the battle existed only in Rónán's grief-crazed mind. Then a rush of blood came out of his mouth and he died.

Feagh McHugh O'Byrne

"the illustrious chief of the tribe of the O'Byrnes" [31]
"that resolute hero and relentless enemy of heretics" [32]
"a base villain ... a dangerous enemy to deal withal" [33]

Feagh M'Hugh of the mountain –
Feagh M'Hugh of the glen –
Who has not heard of the Glenmalur chief,
And the feats of his hard-riding men?
*   *   *   *   *
From Ardamine north to Kilmainham,
He rules, like a king, of few words,
And the Marchmen of seven score castles
Keep watch for the sheen of his swords.
from "Feagh M'Hugh" by T. D. M'Gee [34]

No one during the turbulent last quarter of the 16th century gave the government so much trouble for so long so close to Dublin as Feagh McHugh O'Byrne. The P. J. McCall song "Follow Me Up to Carlow" (see Notes p. 80), a staple in the repertoires of modern ballad groups, celebrates "the insolent outrages and spoils" [35] of one of the last of the great lords – in effect, a local king – of the old Gaelic order.

The O'Byrnes

The O'Byrnes, descendants of Saint Kevin's foster son Fáelán through Bran Mut of the Bórama saga, remained a power to be reckoned with throughout Leinster well into the 16th century, and they still commanded the title "Kings of Uí Fháeláin". "In fact, by their success in maintaining the independence and integrity of their mountainous territory against great odds until the final collapse, [the O'Byrnes] were in a position to attract poets of repute from distant parts of Ireland." [36] (So successful were they that Wicklow was the last county to be officially formed, in

---

[31] O'Byrne, *Historical Reminiscences*, p. 43.
[32] O'Sullivan Bear, p. 97.
[33] Spenser, pp. 116, 117.
[34] Collins, pp. 222-3. Ardamine is in County Wexford; Kilmainham is in West Dublin.
[35] Spenser, p. 20.
[36] Mac Airt, *Leabhar Branach*, p. xiii.

1606.) Two of Feagh's poets, Aonghus mac Doighrí Uí Dhálaigh and Daniel McKeogh, are quoted in this chapter.

During the 16th century, some O'Byrne clans more or less accommodated themselves to English rule and the government policy, enforced by martial law and institutionalised terror, of taking land from the native Irish and giving it to new English colonists. However, "the wily Hugh M'Shane" of the Gabhal Raghnaill clan, which occupied the Ranelagh[37] area roughly from Rathdrum to Shillelagh, continued to resist until his death in 1579, as had his father, Shane McTurlogh. "The Victories of Hugh mac Shane O'Byrne" by his bard Ferganaim M'Keogh records his incursions into the English Pale, the area roughly within a radius of forty miles of Dublin under English control, with the notable exception of the Wicklow Hills.

Hugh's son, Feagh, was named clan leader on Hugh's death, and in 1580 Feagh united the O'Byrnes and allied them with their rivals, the O'Tooles (he married the sister of Phelim O'Toole), a family of Wicklow lords and former kings also descended from Fáelán.

The religious and political background includes the Reformation and Counter-Reformation, England's wars with France and Spain, increased planting of English settlers in Ireland, and persistent prophecies of Ireland's imminent triumph over her oppressors. (See Notes: Feagh McHugh O'Byrne: Background.) Perhaps never before or since were Irish hopes so frequently raised and crushed, and the adages so simultaneously apt: "when England sneezes, Ireland catches a cold"; "England's enemy is Ireland's friend"; "he who England would win, must in Ireland begin".

The Battle of Glenmalure, 25 August 1580

Arthur, Baron Grey de Wilton, arrived in Dublin to take up his post as the new Lord Deputy in August 1580. His secretary was the English poet, Edmund Spenser, author of *The Fairy Queen*, who spent a total of sixteen years in Ireland as a civil servant. Spenser completed his thinly disguised memoirs, *A View of the Present State of Ireland*, in 1596, three years before his death. He served as secretary to Grey from 1580 until Grey's removal at his own request in 1582. (His first request for relief came when he was only four months into the job.) It was Grey who ordered the massacre of the Italians sent by the Pope in 1580. (See Notes: Feagh McHugh O'Byrne: Background.) Spenser described him in *A View* as "most gentle, affable, loving and temperate" and modelled Sir Arthegall in *The Fairy Queen*, which depicts an ideal Ireland, on him.

Immediately upon Grey's arrival he was faced with a crisis. A Catholic landowner in Wicklow, James Eustace, Viscount Baltinglass, who

---

[37] Part of this Ranelagh (var. Ranallach) is near Kilranelagh Hill near Baltinglass, but the two names are not etymologically related. See Notes: Buchet's House.

owned Baltinglass Abbey, declared Queen Elizabeth a heretic and rose in revolt, purportedly backed by the authority of the Pope. He was joined by Feagh McHugh O'Byrne.

As Lord Deputy, Grey wielded near-regal power in Ireland and had direct administrative responsibility for the Pale and Leinster. Although the government's attention was usually concentrated elsewhere – especially on the O'Neill-O'Donnell powder keg in the North – and the O'Byrnes and their allies in Wicklow were normally considered little more than "a conspicuous nuisance" (Spenser), Grey was incensed and embarrassed by a revolt less than 30 miles from Dublin Castle. Conscientious but inexperienced, and perhaps anxious to prove himself, he moved hastily and unwisely.

> Grey said victory was sure –
> Soon The Firebrand he'd secure;
> Until he met at Glenmalure,
>> Feagh MacHugh O'Byrne!
>> *from "Follow Me Up to Carlow"*

The O'Byrne family seat was at Ballinacor next to the modern village of Grianán (Greenan) at the mouth of Glenmalure. A local story tells how a woman used to keep watch from her cottage at the head of the glen. When she saw soldiers approaching she would don a bright red jumper and sit outside her cottage knitting, as a warning to the rebels. But in this case, Feagh had advance information from a deserter, and he knew that the 1000-strong English force was made up largely of raw recruits who were conspicuous in their new red and blue uniforms. On the eve of the battle, Aonghus mac Doighrí Uí Dhálaigh encouraged Feagh's men with a "poem of incitement addressed to the Irish in general, but in particular to the O'Byrnes-Ranallach", beginning:

> God go with you, warrior Gaels,
> May the foreign foemen fail.
> Never have I heard it claimed
> That in battle you were shamed.[38]

Not daring to approach Glenmalure directly through the hostile hills to its southeast-facing open end, Grey took a more secure roundabout route via Naas, through the Glen of Imaal, and over the backbone of the Wicklow Mountains (with an elevation of 690m by the lowest gap), to descend the steep closed northwest end of Glenmalure. This might have been a clever tactic for guerrillas used to the hills, but for Grey's inexperienced infantry and cavalry, it was a disaster. The surrounding terrain and the steep, heavily

---

[38] My translation of the text in Hardiman, p. 280.

wooded sides of this seven-mile-long glen narrowing to a cul-de-sac at its northwest end made it a death trap for government troops.

> The places was such so very ill that were a man never so slightly hurt he was loste, because no man was hable to help him upp the hill. Some died being so out of breath that they were hable to go no further, being not hurte at all.[39]

> When we entered the foresaid glen, we were forced to slide sometimes 3 or 4 fathoms ere we could stay our feet: it was in depth, where we entered, at least a mile, full of stones, rocks, bogs and wood, in the bottom thereof a river full of loose stones, which we were driven to cross divers times. So long as our leaders kept the bottom, the odds of the skirmish were on our side. But our Colonel being a corpulent man not able to endure travail, before we were half through the glen, which was four miles in length, led us up the hill that was a long mile in height: it was so steep that we were forced to use our hands as well to climbe as our feet, and the vanward being gone up the hill, we must of necessity follow: and the enemy charged us very hotly: divers had served among Englishmen ... They were laid all along the wood as we should pass, behind trees, rocks, crags, bogs and in covert.[40]

> And tall amid their foremost band, his broadsword flashing bright,
> The dreaded Feagh MacHugh is seen to cheer them to the fight.
> And from the fiery chieftain's lips these words of vengeance passed,
> "Behold the accursed Sassanach – remember Mullaghmast!"[41]
> *from "The Battle of Glenmalure" by Michael Joseph McCann*[42]

One Irish account puts Grey's losses at 800; another has over 900; government estimates say thirty, probably officers, without counting men.[43] This was the greatest single defeat inflicted on the English during the Irish wars until the 1598 Battle of the Yellow Ford in the North, in which 3000 government troops were killed by combined O'Neill and O'Donnell armies.

> Since which time they [the O'Byrnes and the O'Tooles] are grown to that strength, that they are able to lift up hand against all the state, and now lately through the boldness and late good success of this Hugh

---

[39] Long, p. 248, quoting from an account written shortly after the debacle.

[40] Price, "Notes on Feagh ...", p. 145; quoting Calendar of State Papers ii, 247.

[41] For Mullaghmast see Notes: Feagh McHugh O'Byrne: Background, 1577.

[42] Brown, pp. 95-8.

[43] Price, "Notes on Feagh ...", p. 146. For an excellent account of the battle, see O'Byrne, Emmet, "The Battle of Glenmalure ..."

Upper Lake, Glendalough
(Saint Kevin's Bed, Glendalough, is near centre of photo)

Bullán at the Bridge of the Deer, Glendalough

Elvira at the mouth of
Saint Kevin's Bed, Hollywood

Athgreany Stone Circle, near Hollywood

Feagh McHugh and Michael Dwyer Stone,
near Drumgoff Crossroads, Glenmalure

Sam McAllister's Grave, Kilranelagh Cemetery

Dwyer-McAllister Cottage, near Donard

Avoca Fairy Tree

Thomas Moore Tree, Meeting of the Waters, Avoca
with a bust of the poet in the lower right of the photo

The Mottee Stone, Avoca

The Moving Statue, Avoca

The Spink, Avoca

The Bell Rock, Avoca

Bae Aife, Kilranelagh Hill
(see Fingal Rónáin)

Saint Bridget's Headstone, Kilranelagh Hill

[sic] McHugh they are so far emboldened that they threaten peril even to Dublin, over whose neck they continually hang.[44]

Red Hugh O'Donnell's Escape

See the swords of Glen Imayle
Flashing o'er the English Pale!
See all the children of the Gael
    Beneath O'Byrne's banners!
from "Follow Me Up to Carlow"

Many of those "children of the Gael" who sought sanctuary "beneath O'Byrne's banners" were prisoners who escaped from Dublin Castle and made straight for Glenmalure. One of these, Sir Edmund Butler of Idrone, a friend of Feagh's, repaid his hospitality by having an affair with his wife, Sadhbh. Feagh and Sadhbh separated, she went with Butler, and Feagh married Rose O'Toole. Another escapee, Red Hugh O'Donnell, became the most powerful Ulster chief next to Hugh O'Neill and started the Nine Years' War with his rising in 1594.

On with O'Donnell then! Fight the good fight again!
Sons of Tír Connell are valiant and true!
Make the proud Saxon feel Erin's avenging steel!
Strike! For your Country! O'Donnell abú!
from "The Clan Connell War Song" by Michael Joseph McCann [45]

The story of Red Hugh's escape at the age of 18, featured in all accounts of Feagh and Red Hugh, contains the classic elements of heroism and tragedy. Standish James O'Grady took full advantage of the material in a popular history (or historical novel) called *Red Hugh's Captivity*, which he then streamlined for a boys' adventure version, *The Flight of the Eagle*.

A prophecy was then current that a Hugh who succeeded another Hugh would lead the Irish to freedom (see Notes: Feagh McHugh O'Byrne: Background, 1592). Another prophecy said that a leader with a red mark on his body would rise against the English. Red Hugh, successor to Hugh Manus as The O'Donnell, had such a mark, and so was looked on as a doubly potential saviour. In Irish, he is called both "Aodh Ruadh" (Red Hugh) and "Ball Dearg" (Red Spot). The English kidnapped him in

---

[44] Spenser, p. 117.
[45] c. 1843. Best known as "O'Donnell Abú", the march tune to this song was the sign-on signature tune of RTÉ Radio One from the 1920s until the station began broadcasting 24 hours in the 1990s.

September 1587 when he was 14 and held him for four years in Dublin Castle as a hostage for the behaviour of his father, who they feared would form an alliance with the rival O'Neills.

The first time he escaped, at Christmas 1590, he went to Castlekevin near Annamoe, the home of Phelim O'Toole, the brother of Feagh's wife Rose. Phelim was not in as secure a position as Feagh, being situated within more convenient reach of Dublin, and could not afford to invite trouble by harbouring such a prominent fugitive. Rose, who was at Castlekevin when Hugh arrived, came up with an ad hoc solution. Phelim would pretend to hold Hugh prisoner while a slow message was sent to Dublin Castle and a fast one to Feagh in Glenmalure. The plan was that Feagh would come running and be seen to "force" Phelim to give up Hugh before the Crown forces arrived. "So thou shalt preserve the fugitive, win glory with the great party of which he will one day be the head, and also keep unimpaired thy credit with the Government," Rose says in O'Grady's *Flight*.

Unfortunately, the intervening Avonmore River in the Vale of Clara was swollen with rain, and the messenger to Feagh had to go the long way around, and then Feagh was unable to cross the Avonmore to effect the rescue. So Hugh was captured and locked up again, this time in chains. His cellmates were Art and Henry, sons of Shane O'Neill.

Plans were meticulously laid for the next break, "not without the privity of a great Man, well bribed", who most historians identify as Lord Deputy Fitzwilliam.[46] At the request of Feagh, young Edward Eustace of the house of Baltinglass organised the smuggling into the jail of a metal file to cut the chains, and a bolt of linen, ostensibly for clothing, to be made into an escape rope. Edward also provided four horses, which went missing at the last minute because a friend of his innocently took them away for his own use. Someone, probably Shane O'Neill, though some imply it was Feagh, almost certainly bribed Fitzwilliam to look the other way. According to Standish James O'Grady, Fitzwilliam replaced an able-bodied head jailer with one who was so ill he died two days after the escape. The plan was for the three to make their way quickly out of Dublin to the security of Glenmalure on the horses, and then return to Ulster by a circuitous route.

At Christmas-time 1591, when conditions seemed right, they made their escape. Henry went down the rope first and immediately set off on his own straight for the North. He arrived safely, but then was quickly imprisoned by Hugh O'Neill. Red Hugh descended safely, but Art, who had become "corpulent" and "thick-thighed" and weakened by his long imprisonment, came down too fast and dislodged a stone, which struck and severely injured him. Guided by Edward Eustace, they managed to get out of the city unnoticed and headed for the hills. "The night came on with a drizzle and a violent downpour of rain and slippery slime of snow,"

---

[46] Cox, p. 400, and Morgan, pp. 131-33, among others. See also "Fitzwilliam" in Notes: "Follow Me Up to Carlow".

according to *Beatha Aodha* (The Life of Hugh). Their route is not clear, but they probably went out of Dublin by the southwest and through Tallaght, Bohernabreena and Kilbride to the vicinity of Ballyknockan, which they reached on the second night. They still had 15 miles of rough terrain to go before they reached Feagh's headquarters.

There was deep snow on the ground, and they had inexplicably left their heavy clothing behind. Without horses, the injured Art O'Neill was in poor condition by this time and had to be helped by Hugh and Edward. The arrangement was apparently that they would wait in the hills until it was determined that it was safe to descend into Glenmalure. Hugh and Art took refuge in a cave, while Edward Eustace went alone to investigate the situation. Because of close surveillance, it was two more days before Feagh was able to send help without revealing the boys' presence.

> Alas! unhappy and miserable was [Art and Hugh's] condition on [the arrival of Feagh's men]. Their bodies were covered over with white-bordered shrouds of hail-stones freezing around them on every side, and their light clothes and fine-threaded shirts too adhered to their skin; and their large shoes and leather thongs to their shins and feet; so that, covered as they were with the snow, it did not appear to the men who had arrived that they were human beings at all, for they found no life in their members, but just as if they were dead. They were raised by them from their bed, and they requested of them to take some of the meat and drink; but this they were not able to avail themselves of, for every drink they took they rejected again on the instant; so that Art at length died, and was buried in that place.[47]

"That place" is locally believed to be a depression on Table Mountain called "Art's Grave". Hugh's big toes were frostbitten and had to be amputated, but he survived to start the Nine Years' War two years later.

> In mountain hut and castle keep, bright usquebach [whiskey] doth flow,
> To toast thy health and welcome back our own O'Donnell Roe!
> *from "The Welcome to Hugh Roe O'Donnell" by John Keegan Casey* [48]

---

[47] AFM, at 1592.

[48] Brown, pp. 102-104. The popular Casey (1846-70) is best remembered for "The Rising of the Moon".

The End of Feagh

Feagh harassed the English with frequent bold night raids on Dublin, when cavalry pursuit was impractical, and escaped easily into the protecting hills. Government attempts to build forts and install garrisons in Wicklow were frustrated by unwise dependence on native workmen and troops. The English destroyed Feagh's house at Ballinacor in 1581, but he rebuilt it as a wooden fort surrounded by earthen ramparts and occupied it until he was driven out in January 1595. He was nearly caught that time.

Feagh had been demanding protection money from some of his neighbours, and Lord Deputy Sir William Russell marched on Ballinacor in response to their complaints. The *Annals of the Four Masters* report:

> Upon their arrival in the neighbourhood of the castle, but before they had passed through the gate of the rampart that surrounded it, the sound of a drum was accidentally heard from the soldiers who were going to the castle. Fiagh, with his people, took the alarm; and he rose up suddenly, and sent a party of his people to defend the gate; and he sent all his people, men, boys, and women, out through the postern-doors of the castle, and he himself followed them, and conveyed them all in safety to the wilds and recesses, where he considered them secure.

A fortnight later, Feagh's sons "burned and totally plundered" Crumlin, within sight of the walls of Dublin Castle, in retaliation.

Some historians claim that this was an unprovoked attack on Feagh while he was negotiating with the government for peace, and that it drove him into confederacy with the Ulster lords, Red Hugh O'Donnell and Hugh O'Neill, Earl of Tyrone. Others contend that Feagh was only putting on the appearances of negotiating, while continuing to plot rebellion. In either case, he was soon active again, forcing the government to divert resources from their Ulster campaign. Whenever troops were sent to the North, Feagh harried the Pale south of Dublin. When the English strengthened their positions in Wicklow to draw an effective cordon around Feagh, Ulster erupted. This seems to have been at least partially orchestrated by Feagh and the Ulster lords.

Lord Deputy Russell realised that the Feagh problem required a lasting solution. The English rebuilt Ballinacor immediately as "a verie strong ffortification", but lost it to Feagh the following year. However, the government then refortified and garrisoned castles at nearby Castlekevin and Rathdrum, and cleared mountain passes for the secure movement of troops. Edmund Spenser had suggested this only a year earlier: "... meseems the better course should be by planting of garrisons about him, the which, whensoever he shall look forth or be drawn out with desire of the spoil of those borders or for the necessity of victual, shall be always ready to intercept his going or coming".[49] A similar tactic used against Michael Dwyer in the nearby Glen of Imaal area forced his surrender in 1803.

As was often the case, government policy was split. Russell advocated vigorous action, while his military commander, Sir John Norris, preferred appeasement. Unfortunately for Feagh, who by this time was "unwieldy and spent with years" and had risen again in certain belief that the arrival of Spain's abortive "Second Armada" was imminent, Russell sent Norris to the North and took a direct hand in operations in Wicklow.

Some historians are reticent about the unsavoury and conveniently cloudy episode that probably led to Feagh's downfall. Feagh suspected Turlough, his oldest son, by his first wife, Sadhbh, of being a traitor, based on information given to him by his second wife, Rose, who was in prison and may have been fed false information by the government. Feagh delivered Turlough to the authorities, with this parting speech attributed to him: "Because paternal love will not allow me to inflict fitting punishment for your perfidy, I will give you up to those to whom you would have betrayed me." [50]

Turlough was hanged in chains, protesting his innocence to the end. A short time later, Feagh "was betrayed by one in whom he had complete confidence and who guided the enemy to where they surprised him",[51] apparently a disgruntled member of the immediate family close to Turlough.

On 8 May 1597, three columns converged from separate directions in a lightning attack on Glenmalure, obviously acting on information, and caught Feagh off guard. He was pursued to a cave on Fananierin and trapped. "The fury of our soldiers was so great as he could not be brought away alive," reads the laconic entry in Russell's journal.[52]

Feagh's head was presented to Russell at the scene by the sergeant in charge of the party that had trapped him. His body was then cut into quarters, and his head and quarters placed on the wall of Dublin Castle. The head was later sent to Queen Elizabeth, who threw it away in disgust. After seeing Feagh's head on public display in Dublin, Feagh's poet Daniel McKeogh wrote:

> Woe is me! ah, woe is me! and endless is my grief
> Because I've seen the severed head of my beloved chief;
> Not mine alone the bitter dole; full well may Ireland mourn
> The traitor's blow that laid thee low, brave Feagh MacHugh O'Byrne![53]

---

[49] Spenser, p. 119.
[50] O'Sullivan Bear, p. 76. Kenneth Nicholls ("The Genealogy of the O'Byrnes of Ranelagh", p. 113) suggests that Feagh surrendered Turlough in exchange for Rose.
[51] O'Sullivan Bear, p. 77.
[52] Falls, p. 199.
[53] Sullivan, p. 122. This is Sullivan's translation "from the Gaelic of Daniel McKeogh".

A boulder by the side of the road in Glenmalure near Drumgoff Crossroads[54] and a plaque in the Parnell National Memorial Park in Rathdrum commemorate Feagh today. Phelim McFeagh O'Byrne, Feagh's son by his first wife, Sadhbh, continued the family tradition of insurrection until 1601. In the Battle of Rathdrum, 1599, Phelim routed and killed "the greatest part" of a superior English force of infantry and cavalry. The new Lord Deputy, Charles Blount, Lord Mountjoy, burned his house at Ballinacor on Christmas Eve 1600, but Phelim later built "Phelim's castle", of which no trace remains, on or near the site of the family seat.

> Still proudly over Ballinacor O'Byrne's banner waves;
> And all the Cailliagh Ruad's power, as erst, defiant braves;
> And though heroic Pheagh is gone, well can young Phelim wield
> The sword his sire triumphant waved o'er many a stricken field.
> *from "The Battle of Rathdrum" by Michael Joseph McCann* [55]

Phelim married Úna O'Toole, the sister of Feagh's second wife, Rose, and he became MP for Wicklow in 1613.

---

[54] The boulder is inscribed on both sides in Irish. On one side: "This is the glen in which Feagh McHugh O'Byrne broke battle on the English in AD 1580." On the other side: "In this glen was the stronghold of Michael Dwyer and his warriors in AD 1798."

[55] Brown, p. 119. The "Cailliagh Ruad" (Red Hag) is Queen Elizabeth.

Michael Dwyer

"a troublesome and dangerous ruffian" [56]
"a princely fellow beloved by all" [57]

The Setting

Oh what glorious pride and sorrow fills the name of ninety-eight.
from "The Rising of the Moon" by John Keegan Casey

The rebellion of 1798 was one of the most dramatic events in Irish history. It had a profound effect on religious and political loyalties and influenced the history of Ireland and Anglo-Irish relations into the present [20th] century.[58]

Having suffered more than a century of severe religious and social oppression, and goaded by the examples of the American and French revolutions, Ireland was ripe for rebellion in 1798. For most of the participants, the '98 had nothing to do with political idealism or even independence from British rule. Conditions for Catholics and many Protestants had so deteriorated that most saw open armed rebellion as the only means to ensure their self-preservation.

Wicklow had been in a continual state of turmoil since the beginning of Anglo-Norman colonisation in the late 12th century, and the government was deeply suspicious of the loyalty not only of the Catholic "lower orders", but also of the county's liberal Protestant political establishment. The county was polarized: it had been heavily planted with Anglo-Irish landowners for over a hundred years and contained the highest concentration of Orange Order members outside Ulster; and the United Irishmen, founded in 1791, were actively recruiting the disaffected.

Against '98 broke out they [the United Irishmen] had every man and boy in the Wicklow Mountains that was worth his salt ready for the fight.[59]

---

[56] Bartlett, p. 404, letter from Capt. Myers, Inspector of Yeomanry, Monkstown, to Sir Edward Littlehales, Dublin Castle, 21 June 1803 [NAI 620/66/78].

[57] Cullen, p. 81, summarizing the opinions of the people he interviewed.

[58] From the brochure of the "1798: Fellowship of Freedom" exhibition at the National Museum of Ireland.

[59] Mrs O'Toole in Ó Tuathail, p. 155.

At the first signs of unrest, the Dublin government quickly clamped down on suspected activists with the aid of German Hessian mercenaries, the Antrim Militia and a Welsh cavalry regiment known as the Ancient Britons. The Ancient Britons especially soon earned a reputation for gratuitous brutality similar to that of the 20th-century B-Specials and the Black and Tans. It was the Ancient Britons who committed the Dunlavin and Ballymore-Eustace massacres and are said to have cut out the heart of Father Michael Murphy after the Battle of Arklow and "roasted his body, and oiled their boots with the grease which dripped from it".[60] They got their come-uppance when they were nearly completely wiped out in an ambush at Ballyellis near Carnew on 28 June 1798.

The state terrorism that preceded the Rebellion included arbitrary arrest, random murder and destruction of property, church-burning, house-burning, and systematic and imaginative torture. (See Notes: Michael Dwyer: State Terrorism.) Some believe that this was a deliberate effort on the part of the government to bring matters to a head. Luke Cullen (1793-1859), who interviewed many eye-witnesses of the '98 and its preamble and aftermath, described the situation on the eve of the outbreak of open and organised revolt: "Justice was now suspended, the country was proclaimed, martial law was introduced, and the dictum of beardless officers, unscrupulous and ignorant magistrates, took the seat of law and order." [61]

The Rebellion was effectively crushed on 21 June at Vinegar Hill in Enniscorthy, County Wexford, a month after it started. Heroes of legendary quality were desperately needed by a demoralized people, and Michael Dwyer (1772-1825) filled the role in Wicklow.

> When the star of freedom vanished and our flag went down,
> And the nation's hope was banished from each vale and town,
> Borne intact through blood and fire, Ireland's banner waved again,
> Held aloft by Michael Dwyer and his mountain men.
> *from "Michael Dwyer" by Peadar Kearney* [62]

The "militarily slight but politically significant resistance" [63] of Dwyer and his small band of guerrillas meant that, at least in Wicklow, the Rebellion and the dream of eventual victory lived on until Dwyer's surrender on 14 December 1803.

One of the results that Robert Emmet expected from his romantic but doomed rising in Dublin on 23 July 1803 was the emergence of Dwyer from Wicklow. Emmet was perhaps relying on the fact that his co-conspirator and

---

[60] Madden, *United Irishmen*, Vol. I, p. 238.
[61] Cullen, p. 18.
[62] Faolain, p. 376. Kearney wrote the words to the Irish national anthem, "The Soldiers' Song".
[63] O'Donnell, p. 372.

housekeeper, the heroic Anne Devlin,[64] and Dwyer were first cousins. Emmet sent weapons and ammunition to Dwyer, but Dwyer said he would not involve himself in Emmet's plot unless he saw Dublin in Emmet's hands for 48 hours and the green flag flying above the king's flag on Dublin Castle. During interrogation following his surrender, Dwyer commented, "If Emmet had brain to his education, he'd be a fine man." [65]

Dwyer was born and raised in the Glen of Imaal and rarely ventured out of south and west Wicklow. An intelligent and instinctive tactician, he was in his prime and in good physical condition at the time of the '98. "Dwyer was the cleverest man and there was never a duck hardier on the pond than he." [66] He was intimately familiar with the mountains and bogs of the area, and he knew or was related to many of the inhabitants.

> Micky Dwyer in the mountains to Saunders he owes a spleen,
> For his loyal brothers, who were shot on Dunlavin Green.
> *last two lines of "Dunlavin Green" – Anon* [67]

In addition, the yeomen, mainly Protestant volunteers nominally loyal to the government, respected, feared or even liked him personally. James Hope, an emissary of Emmet, reported:

> Dwyer and his men had a subterraneous retreat in the glen, lined with wood and moss, the entrance to which was covered with a large sod that was cut out of a tuft of heath, where they remained all day, and had their rations as regular as the soldiers in the barracks had, and took to the mountains at night.[68]

It is for these reasons that he was able to remain at large more than five years after the Rebellion in Wicklow officially ended with the surrender of General Holt on 10 November 1798. Most of the stories about him, all supposedly true and many supported by documentary evidence, are set during that period.

---

[64] Ironically, Anne Devlin (1780-1851), from Cronebeg near Rathdrum, was briefly a housekeeper-companion to the wife of Hempenstall in 1797.

[65] Bartlett, p. 406.

[66] Mrs O'Toole in Ó Tuathail, p. 156.

[67] See Notes: Michael Dwyer: The Dunlavin Green Massacre.

[68] Madden, *Emmet*, p. 108.

The Stories

I sing M'Alister, the brave,
Whose deeds are worthy of a song;
To snatch them from oblivion's grave,
And bid them live both late and long.
from "Dwyer and M'Alister: A Tale of 1798" by "G.D." [69]

In the largely neglected graveyard near the top of Kilranelagh Hill,[70] south of the Glen of Imaal and six miles east of Baltinglass, there is a well-tended grave marked "Sam MacAlastair", set off by a wrought-iron fence with symbolic halberd-heads at the corners. On the day after the 200th anniversary of the Derrynamuck incident, I found three bunches of fresh flowers laid on McAllister's freshly tidied grave, and the well-worn path from the hill road to his grave had recently been trodden by a large number of people. McAllister (the usual spelling) was a Presbyterian who had deserted from the Antrim Militia to join Dwyer.

On the night of 15 February 1799, Dwyer and McAllister and ten other men took refuge in three cottages at Derrynamuck on the north slope of Keadeen Mountain on the south side of the Glen of Imaal, after eluding a company of Highlanders in Glenmalure and crossing Lugnaquillia. They were betrayed by a spy, and the cottages were surrounded by at least a hundred soldiers. The eight men in two of the cottages were taken by surprise and arrested before they could offer resistance. One turned informer, and the rest were executed in Baltinglass a few days later.

The weather was wet and the soldiers' powder rendered useless. Ironically, they were only able to exchange fire with the rebels in Dwyer's cottage because they had appropriated the dry powder of the rebels they had captured in the other cottages. Also, until they swooped on the first two cottages, they did not know which cottage Dwyer was in. It was the one furthest from the road.[71]

Dwyer and McAllister and the two men with them in the third cottage were called upon to surrender, but they refused. In the siege that followed, the cottage was set on fire, two of the men were killed, and McAllister was wounded. Knowing that he would not be able to escape, and perhaps suspecting that capture would mean execution, McAllister said to Dwyer:

"I am no use now, and you can't be spared. I will go to the door and discharge the blunderbuss. They will fire at me and you may be off before they load again."

---

[69] *Dublin Penny Journal*, Vol. III, No. 129, December 20, 1834. The stanza quoted is the fourth of 30 "written shortly after the transactions to which they refer had taken place".

[70] Aed Ainmire, the high king who was killed in the Battle of the Pass of Dún Bolg in the Bórama saga, is said to be buried in Kilranelagh Graveyard, as is John Moore (see next chapter).

[71] Oral account from Jim Byrne, Jr, of Rathdangan.

Or in the imagination of an early 19th-century poet:

> "I'll sell my life, to save my friend,"
> Said the noblest blood of Ulster,
> "I'll rush out and dare the Scottish fiends,
> So perish Sam M'Alister.
> And then desperate fire they'll pour on me; ..."
> * * * * * * * *
> But rushing forth from the leader now,
> The hero met their fire,
> And purpled o'er the virgin snow
> To save his Captain Dwyer,
> The persecuted Dwyer.
> *from "On an Escape of Dwyer" – Anon* [72]

McAllister was killed the instant he opened the door. Dwyer made his break and slipped on a patch of ice as he was rounding the corner of the cottage. He stumbled just as a volley was discharged at him. A ball struck him in the clothing, but he was not injured. Half-naked and without shoes or stockings, he set off across the fields, with a Highlander hot on his heels until Dwyer tripped him up. Dwyer said later that if the Highlander had not been so close behind him, the other soldiers would certainly have fired and brought him down.

He quickly out-distanced his pursuers through the heavy snow, but was then sighted by another group of soldiers who had been alerted by the gunshots. Dodging the fire from their muskets and with his bare feet bleeding profusely, he leapt across a swollen branch of the River Slaney, the Little Slaney, just ahead of the soldiers.

They fired as Dwyer landed on the far bank and again slipped and fell. Seeing blood in the snow from his bleeding feet, they thought he had been wounded and would not be able to go far, but the shots had gone over his head and he escaped to trouble the authorities for nearly five more years. [73]

> He baffled his pursuers who followed like the wind;
> He swam the river Slaney and left them far behind.
> But many an English soldier he promised soon should fall
> For those, his gallant comrades, who died in wild Imaal.
> *from "Michael Dwyer" by Timothy Daniel Sullivan ("TD")* [74]

---

[72] Madden, *Literary Remains*, p. 121.
[73] See Notes: Michael Dwyer: The Dwyer-McAllister Incident.
[74] Brown, pp. 229-30. This ballad appears in an 1882 book and survives in oral tradition. Aiden Seerick of County Mayo, who learned it from his mother, can still recite it from memory.

A few weeks later, still recovering from the injuries to his feet, Dwyer was sitting in a chair reading a book outside a friend's house in Imaal near Ballinabarney Gap when a group of soldiers came along unexpectedly. They were too close for any chance of escape, so Dwyer pretended to take no notice of them and continued reading. They passed him by and proceeded to comb the hedges, diligently searching for rebels.

Another time, soldiers approached a house where Dwyer was staying. He took refuge in a piggery behind a large sow. When the searchers came into the piggery, Dwyer poked at the sow from behind to make her stand on her hind legs and roar at the soldiers. They left without completing their search.

Again in Imaal, Dwyer was in a house when he learned that yeoman infantry and cavalry, having been informed that he was there, were approaching from all sides. He changed clothes with an eccentric sympathiser, Augustus Ashmore Fitzgerald, who was well known locally for his outlandish apparel and manner and considered harmless by the authorities. Impersonating the mad Fitzgerald, Dwyer set off along a road and soon encountered a group of the soldiers who were coming to trap him.

He gave a kick to a pig that was in the road, ostensibly to move the animal out of his way, but with the effect of sending it into the ranks of the soldiers, who cursed the supposed mad fool mightily. The captain rounded on the men and forbade them to abuse such an innocent creature. Dwyer was well into the hills before the real Fitzgerald was sighted and the deception discovered.

A neighbour who was supportive of Dwyer was induced to raise the roof of his house just enough to allow for a false ceiling. He was a known sympathiser, and informers several times sent word to the authorities that Dwyer and his men had been tracked to the house and were inside. William Hoare Hume of Humewood near Kiltegan, the liberal MP to whom Dwyer eventually surrendered and whose father had been killed by the Wicklow rebel John Moore, once brought two dozen yeomen to surround and search the house but was unable to find the undetectable low attic where Dwyer and a handful of his men were concealed.

> The next attack was in Keadun bog,
> When they met with Captain Dwyer,
> One hundred cavalry and more
> On him began to fire.
> *from "On Captain Dwyer", ("from L. C.")* [75]

---

[75] Madden, *Literary Remains*, p. 111, who says in a note to this poem: "The affair of Keadun bog is perfectly true, but underrated in the number of the military" (p. 112).

John Thomas Campion's sentimental *Michael Dwyer* ..., characterised by Ruan O'Donnell as "semi-fictional, albeit, highly influential",[76] recounts this adventure in the chapter "The Battle of Kaigeen" (ie, Keadeen Bog).[77]

Dwyer and eight of his men were taking a prisoner at a house near Kilranelagh Hill when they became trapped by 100 Humewood horse and foot, 200 Antrim Militia, and 100 Hacketstown yeomen (Campion's figures) under William Hoare Hume. They took refuge in a ditch. When Hume approached them to request their surrender, Dwyer forced him to back down, and in the resulting uncertainty Dwyer and his men made their way to the rath of "Kresula", a large ancient ringfort called Crossoona Rath on Kilranelagh Hill. After a running fire-fight in which one of his companions was killed, Dwyer and the remaining rebels managed to take refuge in the bog between Kilranelagh Hill and Keadeen, set alight a cottage and barn, and escape in the smoke.

Mrs O'Toole of Ballycumber, Ballinglen, was eight years old when her grandfather, Larry Byrne, one of Dwyer's closest companions, died. She recorded part of her family's oral history on an Ediphone in 1934 for the Irish Folklore Commission, a year before her death at the age of 86. Here are the stories in her own words of two of Dwyer's escapes:[78]

> On one occasion Dwyer and my grandfather and Hugh Byrne of Monaseed and poor McAllister – I am troubled to the heart when I think of poor McAllister; he was a true man – well, the four of them were in a cave on Lugnaquilla when the daylight came. ... So the four awoke, and they began to talk, and they got up and struck their flints and steel 'cause there was no matches. Then they lit their pipes, each of them, and they commenced to smoke and to talk as happy as the day is long, when a robin came in – and a robin is unusual so high up in the mountain, you know – a robin flew in, and she jumped around the quilt over them, and one grabbed at her, and another, and she flew out from the whole of them, and it wasn't two minutes till she came in again, and when she came in she bustled and set herself just as if she was going to jump at them, and she got wicked looking and: "O!" says they, "there is something in this." [79] The four jumped to their

---

[76] Cullen, p. 3. However, most of Campion's stories are merely dressed-up versions of essentially factual incidents.

[77] Campion, pp. 23 ff. "Kaigeen" is a local pronunciation. I have heard "Kay-geen" on the west side of Keadeen Mountain, where this incident occurred, and "Kay-deen" on the east side. Dickson's version is similar, though somewhat less colourful and without giving exact numbers. A woman who lives near the site of the encounter has found a tunnel on Kilranelagh Hill, which she believes Dwyer and his men used in the escape.

[78] Ó Tuathail, pp. 174-6.

[79] The men may have taken this as an omen: "If a robin perched in front of someone, that person might expect some important news or some important letter." (O'Sullivan, Patrick V., p. 35)

feet, and one of them put his head through the hole and he pulled back excited. "O!" he says, "the hillsides is red with soldiers." "Which will we lie in," says another, "or will we get out? If they have bloodhounds we're found out." "That's right," says they, and they all jumped to their feet, and the bloodhounds came in to the bed, but they dragged on their breeches and put their hat on them, and out they went with their guns. Dwyer whipped his sea-whistle and he whistled, and he could be heard, I suppose, in Arklow, and they fired off their three shots, and the soldiers turned around and they ran for their lives, and they never got time to look back till they fell over Lugnaquilla, and they told when they got below that the hills was full of rebels.

One Sunday morning Dwyer and McAllister were at Mass in Knockananna Chapel,[80] and they brought their guns with them and left them by the wall. The priest remonstrated with them and said that the House of God was no place to bring guns, but McAllister who was a Presbyterian but used to go to Mass with Dwyer said: "It is not always we have a rebellion, Father. Go on with the Mass!" And the priest did so.

During the Mass a neighbour came to Dwyer and said that he had been at the window and that the chapel yard was full of soldiers, and Dwyer picked out two clever young fellows and he told them for to go away to a field a distance from the chapel-yard but in sight of it, and says he, "Take off your coats."

He told them to run along the field in their shirts as fast as they could, and he picked out two or three more young chaps of boys that were clever enough to understand him, and he told them to go down beside the soldiers and stand looking at this field and to cry out each one in surprise and wonder: "There they go! There they go!" And they did so, and the soldiers asked them who did they mean by there they go, and they told them – all cried out: "Dwyer and McAllister! Dwyer and McAllister!" The soldiers started for to overtake Dwyer and McAllister, and they failed on it for Dwyer and McAllister was hid in the chapel and when the soldiers cleared out they cleared out and went their way in peace and quietness. The soldiers went out across the fence and they came on the two boys that ran, and they sitting with their coats on, and they smoking their pipes, and they asked them did they see two men running through the fields, and they said "No," that they were not long there. So Dwyer and McAllister walked off in safety and left the poor lads wandering about to look for them.

---

[80] Dickson (p. 132) agrees with current tradition in Rathdangan that the "Knockananna Chapel" incident happened in Rathdangan.

A disabled man called "Billy in the Bowl", who "hobbled along, sitting in a wooden bowl, on hand-stools", overheard a plot by Dwyer and two of his men to let soldiers surround Dwyer in Kevin's Bed in Glendalough so that Dwyer's men could surround and trap the soldiers. The soldiers were not aware of the cave situated in a vertical cliff on Lugduff above the Upper Lake, and when Billy led them to the spot and pointed out the cave, Dwyer "let fly at him, and he blew him out of the old box".[81]

> The commander ordered the soldiers to enter, but several were hurled back dead into the lake. An order was given to procure timber for rafts and scaling ladders; but when it arrived, it was found that the bird had flown, having, under cover of darkness, scaled the rocks above the Bed.[82]

Now that the government knew Kevin's Bed was one of Dwyer's bolt-holes, they sent in a troop of Highlanders to root him out. Sergeant Donald M'Bane, "one of the best shots that ever rammed down a bullet", caught sight of Dwyer at the Bed, fired, and gave him a grazing wound.

> [Dwyer] thought it high time for him to bolt, and so, naked so that he might run light, he took to his well-known pass up the face of Lugduff. The Highlanders, like sporting fellows, immediately grounded their muskets, and, bayonets in hand, started off in pursuit: some making after him by the head of the lake, towards Gleneola; others turned to the left, and made their way over the stream by Polanass. In the meantime Dwyer was toiling up the face of the mountain, and they could see a streak of blood running from shoulder to flank, and down the white limbs of the clean-skinned fellow; when half way up the hill, he turned round to look after the Scotchmen, and saw that all had turned either to the right or left of the lake in making towards him, and had left the whole of Comaderry side without a man. Dwyer at once changed his plan, bounced and bounded down the face of the hill, plunged into the lake at Templenaskellig, swam across the water before you could say Jack Robinson, and took possession of all the Scotchmen's muskets and cartridge boxes – and now maybe it was not he that shouted, and crowed, and triumphed, as one after another he pitched the guns and ammunition into the lake; you could hear his huzzas rattling and echoing through the hills, as if the mountains clapped hands with joy, and tossed the triumph from one to another; he then very leisurely lounged away towards

---

[81] Mrs O'Toole in Ó Tuathail, p. 176.
[82] O'Kelly, p. 337. See Notes: Saint Kevin and Glendalough for a description of the Bed.

Toulenagee mountain, and so off towards his old haunts under Lugnaquilla.[83]

Dwyer's Surrender

By 1803, their failure to capture Dwyer had so embarrassed the authorities that they took extraordinary measures to make his situation untenable. The network of military roads, begun around the country during agitations before the '98, was expanded in South Wicklow; more army barracks were planned for the area;[84] Dwyer's family and associates were arrested; and soldiers were billeted in civilians' homes. William Hoare Hume, who probably knew Dwyer better than anyone else on the government side, said in a letter dated less than two months before Dwyer's surrender, "I am now certain that no consideration whatsoever will induce Dwyer or his associates to surrender." [85] However, the intensive military occupation of his home ground and the neutralising of his infrastructure meant Dwyer had no hope of surviving the coming winter.

There are conflicting accounts of the conditions under which Dwyer agreed to surrender and what actually happened after his surrender. One source says that he was promised £500 and to be allowed to emigrate to the United States with his family. Another says:

> In 1803 Dwyer, with two companions, surrendered to Mr. Hume, and the Government of the day promised Mr. Hume free pardon for them, Dwyer to receive £500, the others £200 each, and all to be allowed to emigrate. When Mr. Hume brought them to Dublin Castle, this offer was traitorously withdrawn. The three men were lodged in Kilmainham Gaol, whence they were transported. Mr. Hume was so incensed at this betrayal that he challenged the Lord Lieutenant to a duel, but he declined to fight, as he was the representative of His Majesty in Ireland.[86]

Campion puts the following speech into Hume's mouth on the Lord Lieutenant's reneging on the terms of the surrender of Dwyer and his companions: "I deeply regret I did not leave the men free on the mountains where I found them, and where your Lordship dared not seek them." [87]

---

[83] *The Dublin Penny Journal*, Vol. III, No. 123, November 8, 1834, pp. 150-1.

[84] This is the tactic advised by Edmund Spenser in 1596 to isolate and capture the elusive Feagh McHugh O'Byrne. See Notes: Michael Dwyer: The Military Roads.

[85] William Hoare Hume to Alexander Marsden, 21 October 1803 (Cullen, p. 182).

[86] O'Kelly, pp. 336-7.

[87] Campion, p. 127.

Luke Cullen adds a full pardon for Dwyer and four others to the conditions demanded and accepted, but without the family stipulation and the duel: "... Dwyer repeated his conditions, and Mr. Hume repeated the words, and said, 'I am authorised to accept of your surrender on those conditions.'" [88] However, on his arrival at Dublin Castle Dwyer was arrested for high treason. Cullen says that after more than a year's incarceration in Dublin, Dwyer was transported to Australia, not making it clear whether his wife accompanied him.

Campion says Dwyer's wife, Mary, accompanied him to Australia, but their children did not arrive until after his death.

In Mrs O'Toole's version, Dwyer was persuaded by neighbours to meet with Hume at Imaal (Ballinabarney) Gap after dark:

> ... and when they were drawing near Hume got a bit shaky about Dwyer and he cried out: "Was that Dwyer?" and Dwyer said it was, and he asked him: "Dwyer have you got arms on you?" "I have," says Dwyer, "but they won't affect you tonight." So they drew near to each other, and Hume mentioned a number of transports abroad, but Dwyer told him if he made up his mind to go anywhere he'd go where he liked, and if not he'd stay at home and give them more of it. Hume, delighted to hear of a chance of getting shut of him at all, to get him out of Ireland, threw up his arms and he said: "All right, Dwyer, all right. Go where you please. We'll send you anywhere."
>
> So Dwyer said he'd go to Sydney in Australia, and if they did not send him there he'd go nowhere at all but would stay at home and give them more of it. So they sent him to Sydney in Australia, and he brought his pike along with him. [89]

In a recent summary of Dwyer's career, Thomas Bartlett states that he was transported to Australia in July 1805 and was joined by his wife and children the following year. In a note in the Cullen book, Ruan O'Donnell adds that Dwyer arrived in Australia in February 1806, became a constable and then a high constable, and eventually opened a pub called "Harrow Inn".

Dwyer's brother, Hugh, said that Dwyer's wife went with him to Australia. "His children did not go out for many years after his transportation; he sent for them shortly before his death, but when they arrived, he was not living." [90]

Dwyer's great-grandson and great-great-grandson visited Wicklow in 1998 and are reported to have said that Dwyer's wife Mary and their

---

[88] Cullen, pp. 117-19.
[89] Ó Tuathail, pp. 177-8. It is unlikely that Dwyer took a "pike", that is, a halberd, or would have been allowed to. He "never knew a pike to have any effect but against a prisoner" and preferred "a musket by day and a blunderbuss by night" (Bartlett, p. 407).
[90] Madden, *Emmet*, p. 116.

children did not go to Australia with him or join him there, and that they themselves were the descendants of Dwyer and his Australian wife.[91]

A monument to the "Wicklow Chieftain" erected in 1898 is said to be the largest memorial in Sydney today.[92]

---

[91] Oral account from Mrs Whittle of Donard.
[92] *Wicklow Commemorating 1798-1998*, p. 20.

The Hanging of John Moore
(and the Desecration of a Holy Well)

It is with heartfelt concern that we announce the death of Captain Hume, one of the Members in Parliament for the co. Wicklow, who was killed [8 October, near Rathdangan] in an action which his corps has had with Holt's ferocious banditti. He had been all the preceding night at the head of this corps, and a part of the army, in search of Holt, when returning home to take some rest, and considerably in front of his party, when he came up with some of Holt's party, whom he mistook for some of his friends, as they were dressed in the military fashion, and was shot through the body and head. The murderers then effected their escape up the mountains.

Dublin Evening Post, *11 October 1798*

[Hume saw men in uniform and got close before he discovered they were not his own troops.] One of the desperate villains, who was dressed in an officer's outside coat, at this moment drew forth a pistol, the ball from which entered the Captain's side, and being brought to the ground by the wound, another of the party shot him through the head in view of the corps, who thus saw their officer massacred without its being possible, from their distance, to offer that instant aid which his situation rendered necessary.

Courier Newspaper, *15 October 1798* [93]

[John O'Neill] also told me he saw Mr. Hume, a captain of the cavalry shot. I asked him how he was situated; he said he had left his horse and ran up the hill. I told him I did not doubt the truth of his statement, that Captain Hume was always a coward. ...

I then got an account from John Moore, one of my cavalry, of the death of Mr. Hume, as follows: – Captain Hume was a little in advance of his corps, when Moore met him, and presented his piece at him, well knowing who he was. He cried out, "Cavalry-man, I am Captain Hume, what party do you belong to?"

Moore replied, "General Holt's; and if you put your hands to your pistols, I will blow your brains out, dismount this instant." Captain Hume then dismounted, and when on the ground Moore shot him through the head with a pistol. The troops appeared in a few minutes and began to fire, and my brother [Jonathan] was killed before they retreated.

from the memoirs of Joseph Holt, a leader of the 1798 insurgents in Wicklow [94]

---

[93] Quoted by Croker, pp. 352-3.

John O'Neale swore that the party of rebels to which he belonged, was closely pursued by the King's troops, through Glenmalure into Aughavanagh, where they saw different parties of the King's troops in pursuit of them. They had but six horsemen of their party, three in red, and three in coloured clothes. Captain Hume having mistaken them for a party of yeomen, advanced near them and cried out, – "Is there not enough to mind that position?" Conway, one of the rebels, asked him, "who he was?" to which he answered, "Captain of a corps of cavalry." Conway then said, "Did you ever hear of the Ballynatrochin[95] cavalry?" and then raising his firelock missed-fire at him. On which Moore shot him, and mounted his horse, and Conway took his spurs.

testimony at the trial of John Moore [96]

John Moore was a young carpenter from Arklow and a deserter from the Antrim Militia. His father was driven from his property near Arklow by yeomen, and he moved to the Kiltegan area, where he opened a sheebeen (an unlicensed pub) at Tynock near Killalish, about two miles from William Hume's Humewood estate. Hume, magistrate and captain of the Upper Talbotstown yeomen cavalry, had the pub shut down, and the senior Moore was fined £10 (about €1300). Impoverished by the loss of his property, Moore was unable to pay the fine, and a friend had to pay for him. The son, John, was said to hold a grudge against Hume for his action.

The above reports show the encounter to have been part of a military engagement, and according to the rules of war Hume should have been considered a prisoner after he apparently surrendered by dismounting. The summary execution of prisoners was carried out by both sides, although since the government forces were better placed to take and hold prisoners, more rebels were killed in this way than official troops.

Local tradition insists the murder was a personal act of vengeance. The story current in Rathdangan is that Moore took Hume's gun from him and killed him with it. Also, that Moore was a violent man who had on at least one occasion been prevented by Michael Dwyer from killing an innocent Protestant.

All accounts agree that after the murder Moore went to Dublin and worked as a carpenter for some time under an assumed name and that O'Neill informed on him, presumably collecting the reward: £500 put up by the Hume family, £500 by the government, and several hundred raised by

---

[94] Croker, pp. 252-3.

[95] This may be an attempt at sardonic humour. The incident occurred in or on the border of the townland of Ballyknockan. "Ballynatrochin" is not recorded as a place-name in Wicklow. The Irish word *troch* (var. *truán / truaghán*) means "miserable person, wretch"; "*trocha*" is a literary term for "doom, untimely death" (Ó Dónaill, *Foclóir*).

[96] Reported by Sir Richard Musgrave, Croker, pp. 252-3n.

local subscription.[97] A local man, Thomas Whitty, was hanged in Ballinguile for refusing to inform on Moore.

According to testimony given by Michael Kearns at Moore's trial, Moore and others came across Hume riding alone at Ballinabarney Gap,[98] between Rathdangan and the Glen of Imaal. Hume was well known to be friendly with the local residents, even those he must have suspected of being rebels or sympathisers, and Kearns expected the parties to pass without incident, but

> as [Hume] got alongside of [Moore] he suddenly seized Moore's musket, and exultingly said "I have you at last, Moore." ... Moore entreated him quietly to let go his musket, but he held it the more firmly. He entreated him again, but perceived that entreaties were in vain. He was conscious of his superior strength and dexterity to wrest it from his assailant at any moment notwithstanding that Mr Hume was a strong and resolute man. At length he did, cocked it and shot him through the head.[99]

John Campion's characteristically lurid and "exact account, and nearly in Moore's own words, of the manner in which he committed the crime," contradicts some key points of that version:

> I had been in ambush for many weeks in the plantations of Humewood, waiting for my man, but never got a glimpse of him until the very day of his death. On that day, I and six of my followers were in the house of a tenant of Mr. Hume's, when it was suddenly announced to us that a strong body of the military was advancing in our direction, and was not far distant. Upon the word we all rushed out, intending to seek, at once, a place of security, but had not gone far when we saw a gentleman in coloured clothes riding on the side of the hill.
>
> "Hullo!" he cried, as he observed us (some of us, too, being in uniform). "To what regiment do you belong?" Neill (who afterwards turned informer) gruffly replied – "We don't belong to you – whoever you are!" "I am Mr. Hume of Humewood." "The devil, you are!" said I; "then you are the very man I have long been waiting for."
>
> So saying, I rushed on him and dragged him from his horse, before he could free his pistol from the holsters. He caught my musket, but I called on Neill to shoot him. Neill snapped his gun, but it missed fire, and he ran away. The struggle was now between Mr. Hume and myself; I tripped him up quickly, however, and whilst

---

[97] Drury, p. 330. See Notes: The Hanging of John Moore: The Reward.
[98] See Notes: The Hanging of John Moore: The Hume Stone.
[99] Dickson, pp. 389-90.

falling disengaged my musket from his grasp, then falling back a few paces I cried out – "By G--, I'll shoot you," upon which I fired, and the contents lodged in his stomach.

Falling on his back, he exclaimed, "Ah, spare my life, and I will obtain your pardon, and a commission for you in the army."

"You can do nothing for me," I answered; "I am a deserter, and can expect neither reward nor mercy." I then mounted his horse, but seeing the wounded man rising on his knees, I drew a pistol from his holster, and, stooping down over him, fired and blew off his skull.[100]

After Moore was sentenced on 10 June 1799 to be hanged, he accused O'Neill of the murder: "As God is my judge, I was not within 150 Perches [about half a mile] when he was shot by the Prosecutor O'Neile." [101] Hume's son, William Hoare Hume (to whom Michael Dwyer surrendered in 1803), is reported to have approached Moore as he was about to be hanged:

"Moore! You are going to die," said he in a very gentle tone, "but before you leave this world, tell me truly, are you the man who murdered my father?" Moore looked down quietly, and distinctly replied: "All I will say is, never put any *other* man to death for him."[102]

Moore was hanged in Rathdangan on 13 June "from an ash-tree, now [1908] dead, over the well called Tubberowen" [*Tober Eoin* – "Saint John's Well"].[103] The tree was cut down about 1924, and the stump remained until at least 1944. A "patron" (or "pattern", an annual religious ceremony) was held at the well on Saint John's Eve, 23 June, until the tree was used for Moore's execution. Accounts survive of how the tree used to be festooned with pieces of cloth and sticks and crutches in the manner of holy wells elsewhere in the country. The limb on which Moore was hanged decayed and "never had a green leaf on it afterwards". The tree was eventually blown down, but when the decayed branch was used for firewood, it exploded.[104]

Campion's graphic account of the aftermath of the hanging is confirmed by other sources as essentially factual. Campion says that Moore's body was subsequently decapitated, drawn and quartered and taken by Orange yeomen, apparently members of Hume's Upper Talbotstown troop, and left to hang for a fortnight on a gibbet nearby "on the bounds of [the townlands of] Carrig and Muckduff, where a mound of stones still

---

[100] Campion, pp. 32-3.

[101] Dickson, p. 133.

[102] Dickson, p. 134.

[103] Drury, p. 330.

[104] O'Toole, p. 123.

marks the site, and is named Moore's Gibbet".[105] This so distressed his widow that two Protestants took the remains down and buried them. The Orangemen disinterred the body and re-erected it on the gibbet. Moore's widow appealed to the late Mr Hume's daughter, who arranged for the body to be buried in the graveyard on Kilranelagh Hill.

Saint John's Well can be seen in Rathdangan, about 50 feet down a lane off the left of the road about 100 yards north of the crossroads. No cures are reported associated with the well today, and until piped water became available, it was used for drinking water. Both are signs that the well has not been considered holy for some time. A Celtic cross was erected in 1948 near the well with a banner engraved "Creideam agus Tír" (Creed and Country) wrapped around a halberd, and the inscription:

> I ndíl-cuimne ar
> Sean O Morda
> agus laocra an Ceanntair seo
> a troid agus dfulaing an bas
> ar son na hEireann
> sa bliain 1798
> agus mar cuimneacan
> orta siud
> a lean a lorg o soin.

> (In dear memory of
> John Moore
> and the heroes of this District
> who fought and suffered death
> for the sake of Ireland
> in the year 1798
> and as a memorial
> for those
> who followed in their footsteps.)

---

[105] O'Kelly, p. 336. This is not "The Pinnacle", a heap of stones which can be seen from the well. Moore's Gibbet is further west, on Carrig.

HEPENSTALL
the walking Gallows

With this Month's Publication we give a Likeness of the infamous Lieutenant HEPENSTAL, better known as the WALKING GALLOWS, in the act of Hanging a poor Peasant.

The Irish Magazine, January 1810

Hempenstall – "The Walking Gallows"

Amongst the monsters which the Insurrection Act, passed in 1796, called into loyal activity, none have surpassed *"the Walking Gallows"* for atrocity.
The Irish Magazine, *January 1810* [106]

Lieutenant Edward Lambert Hepenstal (known as "Hempenstall" in Wicklow oral tradition) was born about 1776 in Upper Newcastle, County Wicklow, and "bred an apothecary" in Dublin.

Towering almost to seven feet [*The Irish Magazine* says "7½ feet"], with chest and muscles in proportion, [he] dispensed with the formalities of assembling juries and erecting gibbets, and on encountering a supposed criminal threw a rope round his neck, and swung him over his own shoulders, as he would have done a young deer or a rabbit, there to dangle till he was dead.[107]

He was given a commission in the Wicklow Militia through the influence of his brother, a clerk with the Dublin police, and commanded a "flying party" to Moyvore or Mysores in Westmeath in 1796, where he simultaneously hung two brothers from his shoulders. He killed six men in cold blood in Gardenstown and Moyvore in 1797.

In 1795, Hepenstal half-hanged a prosecution witness named Hyland to encourage him to give false evidence against a man for an armed attack. Hyland retracted his statement in court and was arrested, indicted, convicted, sentenced and hanged on the same day.

During a trial in 1796, Hepenstal admitted that he had not only "used some threats, and pricked him with a bayonet" to obtain testimony from a prosecution witness, but the prisoner himself had also "been pricked with a bayonet, to induce him to confess: a rope had been put around his neck, which was thrown over his (Hepenstal's) shoulder, he then pulled the rope, and drew the prisoner up, and he was hung in this way for a short time, but continued sulky, and confessed nothing".

The defence attorney put it to Hepenstal:

---

[106] The enigmatic and energetic editor/publisher/printer of *The Irish Magazine*, Walter "Watty" Cox, worked as a gunsmith for the government and was suspected of being an informer, a double agent and an agent provocateur or hired denouncer.

[107] Bernard, Vol. I, p. 6.

"Then you acted the executioner, and played the part of a gallows?"

"Yes, please your honour;" was the reply of Lieutenant Hepenstal.

The Solicitor-General, Mr. Toler, who tried the case, in his charge to the jury regretted the treatment of the prisoner, "but it was an error such as a young and gallant officer might fall into, warmed by resentment." ... The prisoner was found guilty.[108]

The Irish Magazine, a racy Dublin nationalist monthly branded "scandalous" and "scurrilous" by its detractors, reported that Hepenstal died in bed in St Andrews Street in Dublin in 1804 "of the most shocking distemper: his body was literally devoured by vermin; and the agonies of his sufferings were aggravated by the most awful expressions, declaring the tortures of a soul apparently surrounded with all the impatient messengers of hell ..." (continuing in a similar vein). He was buried in St Andrews Street, but "so secretly has the spot been concealed, lest some disloyal hand should violate the valuable shrine, that no enquirer, however ingenious, could accurately say, 'Here lies the Walking Gallows!'" [109]

However, Mrs O'Toole, whose grandfather Larry Byrne was a companion of Michael Dwyer, reported in 1934 that Hepenstal was killed along with two companions in Aghavannagh about 1798 when he attacked a group of rebels. She said he is buried "across from Aghavannagh" with flagstones at his head and feet to show his size.[110]

Here lie the bones of Hepenstal,
Judge, jury, gallows, rope, and all.
(by "a clerical gentleman of the name of Barrett") [111]

A local tradition says that Hepenstal hanged his last man at the gate to the Aghavannagh youth hostel, and his gigantic ghost has been seen there during the day by non-local people who had never heard the story before.

---

[108] Madden, *United Irishmen*, Vol. II, pp. 246-7. Toler, who became Lord Chief Justice as Lord Norbury, was "one of the most blackhearted and sadistic scoundrels who ever wore scarlet and ermine", according to Hale, pp. 102-103.

[109] *The Irish Magazine*, January 1810, pp. 1-2.

[110] Ó Tuathail, pp. 163-4.

[111] Madden, *United Irishmen*, Vol. II, p. 247.

The Vale of Avoca

Thomas Moore and the Meeting of the Waters

The Meeting of the Waters
(Air: "The Old Head of Denis")
by Thomas Moore (1779-1852)

There is not in this wide world a valley so sweet
As the vale in whose bosom the bright waters meet;
Oh! the last rays of feeling and life must depart
Ere, the bloom of that valley shall fade from my heart,
Ere, the bloom of that valley shall fade from my heart.

Yet it was not that Nature had shed o'er the scene,
Her purest of crystal and brightest of green,
Oh! no, it was something more exquisite still,
Oh! no, it was something more exquisite still.

'Twas that friends, the belov'd of my bosom, were near,
Who made every dear scene of enchantment more dear,
And who felt how the best charms of nature improve,
When we see them reflected from looks that we love,
When we see them reflected from looks that we love.

Sweet vale of Avoca, how calm could I rest,
In thy bosom of shade with the friends I love best,
Where the storms that we feel in this cold world should cease,
And our hearts, like thy waters, be mingled in peace,
And our hearts, like thy waters, be mingled in peace.

"The Meeting of the Waters" forms a part of that beautiful scenery which lies between Rathdrum and Arklow, in the county of Wicklow; and these lines were suggested by a visit to this romantic spot in the summer of the year 1807.
Moore's footnote, Irish Melodies, *1808*

The Glendassan River out of that glen and the Glenealo River from Glendalough join the Avonmore from Lough Dan, and where the Avonmore joins the Avonbeg from Glenmalure to form the Avoca River is the famed "Meeting of the Waters" of Moore's poem. A bust of the poet and a dead tree commemorate the poem in the public park opposite the pub called "The Meetings". Local legend has it that Moore composed the poem while sitting under the then living tree, but his wife later admitted that he had written it at their home in Brompton. It was first published in the first number of *Irish Melodies*, 1808. Locally, this meeting of rivers is called the "first meeting", the "second meeting" being some four miles downstream at Woodenbridge where the Aughrim, newly augmented by the Goldmine, joins the Avoca River, which then continues to Arklow where it empties into the Irish Sea. Some local people argue that the second meeting is the subject of the song.

A statue of Moore stands over a now-closed men's public toilet next to Trinity College in Dublin. A brass plaque set into the footpath in front of the statue quotes from page 133 of James Joyce's *Ulysses*: "He crossed under Tommy Moore's roguish finger. They did right to put him up over a urinal: meeting of the waters."

One day Thomas Moore and a friend were standing at the Meeting of the Waters admiring the view. A beggar came up to them looking for money, but Moore ignored him. The beggar said:

> "If Moore was a man without place of abode,
> Without clothes on his back, and him walking the road,
> Without bit in his belly or shoes on his feet,
> He wouldn't give a damn where the bright waters meet."

Moore asked him to repeat it, and he did. "That's as good as I ever heard," said Moore. "I couldn't do better myself." And he gave him half a sovereign.[112]

These are some of the stories I heard and experienced when I lived in the Vale of Avoca during the 1980s.

Bob Pyne

Bob Pyne, who lived near The Meetings pub, was a seasonal agricultural worker by day and a well-loved amateur singer in local pubs in the evenings. He sang old music hall and traditional songs, as well as some of his own composition. A moderate drinker, he would gesture during his performance with his trademark small bottle of Guinness, always ending with a shy grin. He has been greatly missed since he died at the age of 61 in 1987.

As a local pet character – I never heard a harsh word from or about him – Bob was the subject of many stories. His mother had been "silenced by the priest", they say. There are two interpretations of what this meant. One is that his mother had "seen something" and had been told by the priest not to speak of it. The other is that she had a sharp tongue, and the priest told her not to speak at all for her penance. Whatever the reason, she was

---

[112] Told to Glassie, op. cit., by Peter Flanagan of Fermanagh, 1972.

thought by one local boy, Mick Howlett, to be dumb. He told me years later how he was shocked when he discovered that she was not.

"One day she said to me, 'You're Tom Howlett's son, aren't you?' and I nearly fell over, because I had never heard her speak before."

Bob's mother was also said to be "touched", that is, touched by the fairies. Bob was likewise believed to be touched – he was called the King of the Fairies, though not to his face – and two stories are told in illustration.

One day, a local man was standing in the doorway of The Meetings pub waiting for the heavy rain to let up enough so that he could dash to his car. He saw Bob Pyne get out of a car near the bridge over the Avonbeg, about 50 feet from the pub, and walk toward the pub. As Bob passed him in the narrow entrance, the man noticed that Bob did not have a drop of rain on him, and he had not been carrying an umbrella.

"Why did you not ask Bob how he managed to stay dry in the rain?" said one of the man's friends when he told the story.

"I didn't want to be asking, because I was afraid of what he might be telling me."

Another time, a man was walking along the narrow back road where Bob lived near The Meetings when he saw Bob, whom he knew well, walking down the road towards him. They said Hello to each other and went on their separate ways. A quarter of a mile further along the road, the man saw Bob walking toward him again. There was absolutely no way Bob could have doubled back in the time between the two sightings.

I said to Bob one time, "I hear some queer stories about you. What do you think of them?" Bob replied, "Ah, you don't want to believe everything you hear." But he never denied them. Or offered an explanation.

The Avoca Non-leprechaun

Mick Howlett reports that when he was about 10 he and some friends were out snaring rabbits one day, and they saw a creature running away through the underbrush on two legs. It was not a rabbit or a hare, and Mick is adamant that he and his friends never claimed it was a leprechaun, though others may have used that term. They knew what they saw, they all saw it, and they had never seen anything like it before or since.

The Tigroney Ghost

In 1980-1, I lived at Tigroney House[113] (formerly Cherrymount) just outside the village of Avoca. At the time it was a community of writers and artists. A friend of mine was in the large communal kitchen in the Big

---

[113] See Notes: The Vale of Avoca: Tigroney House.

House – part of which is some 300 years old – preparing breakfast one day about noon. She saw a male figure pass by the kitchen door wearing a brown robe with a hood over his head. This would not have been unusual garb for some of the residents, but she didn't recognise him, and she wanted to introduce herself to what she assumed was a visitor or a new resident. It took her perhaps ten seconds to cross the kitchen from behind the counter to the doorway. When she looked into the hall, she could see no one. She checked the nearby rooms and outside the house and found no trace of the stranger. She asked the other residents if there had been a new arrival or visitor, but there hadn't. She told me about the incident, and it remained a mystery to be enhanced at the garden party a few months later.

Residents and friends from outside the community were gathered for a tea party on the lawn next to the drawing room one fine summer evening. A young woman visitor saw a male figure wearing a brown robe with a hood over his head pass across the lawn in the growing dusk and slowly vanish into thin air. She insisted that he had not walked out of sight behind a tree or bush. All residents and visitors were accounted for, and no one had been wearing anything like the costume she described.

Some time later I stumbled across the information that solved the mystery to the satisfaction of most of the residents, although the owner of the house once said, apropos of nothing: "About that ghost – there is no ghost here." It seems that the site had once been occupied by a Franciscan monastery.

The Cherrymount Fairy

The 1987 *Avoca Local History Guide* tells about an encounter two local girls had "many years ago" with "a very pretty woman all dressed in white, and sitting on the stump of a tree" in the woods near Tigroney House when it was still called Cherrymount. "She was very small and kept smiling at them and beckoned to them to come closer," but they ran away. One of the girls, a woman still living in the area in 1987, said she believed the little woman was either a fairy or the Blessed Virgin.

The Avoca Púca

In his *Place-names of Co. Wicklow*, Liam Price comments on the place-name "The Black Dog" on the Vale Road (R752) between Avoca Village and Woodenbridge: "The name is not in the Name Book. Perhaps it was originally the name of an inn." [114] Perhaps, but if so, how did the inn get its name? People who live along that stretch of the road say that a large

---

[114] Price, *Place-names*, p. 464.

black dog with fiery red eyes is frequently seen in the area. This is the normal form taken in the South of Ireland by the type of fairy or Otherworld creature or elemental known as a *púca*, (Anglicised "pooka"). In the North and in Britain, the púca is usually a horse-like creature. (See Miscellaneous Tales: A Redcross Púca and Poulaphuca.)

"Me and Thee"

John Keogh, who lived up the hill north of Avoca Village, used to tell the shortest ghost story I've ever heard. One evening, he and his wife went to visit her sister, who lived nearby. John was bored and announced he was going home, but told his wife she could stay as long as she liked. He went home and stoked up the fire. He had just taken one of his wellies off, when he heard a voice: "Now, John, there's only me and thee in the house."

John said, "As soon as I get this boot back on, there'll only be thee."

He quickly did and there soon was.

The Mottee Stone

The Mottee Stone is an erratic granite boulder about 12 feet in diameter left perched by the last glacier on top of Cronebane next to abandoned copper mine workings north of the village and east of the Meeting of the Waters. Fionn mac Cumhaill used to stand on Tara Hill in Wexford, about 15 miles to the south, and throw quoits over it, so they say. A man from the area has told me he understood that Cúchulainn used the Mottee Stone for a *sliotar* (hurling ball). I lived for a time across the Avoca River from Moore's shop and pub near the White Bridge. This is close to the path the Mottee Stone takes every First of May when it rolls down to the river for a drink. No one knows for sure what the name "Mottee" means, but as the stone is halfway between Dublin and Wexford Town, and the French language came into Ireland with the Anglo-Normans in the 12th century, the most reasonable guess is that it comes from the French word *moitié*, meaning "halfway".

The Fairy Tree

There is a sharp left bend around an open field in the road up the hill from the White Bridge to Cronebane and the Mottee Stone (not the rutted track running past the abandoned mine workings). Just before you turn, if you look straight ahead you will see a majestic sycamore, the Fairy Tree, in the middle of the field. The road bends there to give the tree a wide berth, I am told, because no one would dare to cut it down. There are several stories of bad luck coming to people who interfered with the tree. A young man told me that he broke his arm when he fell while climbing the tree a few years ago, for example, although that may be discounted as a fairly normal childhood accident. A more severe punishment was inflicted on the family of a man who cut branches from it, but as the family is still living in the area, I have been asked not to publish the details. Suffice it to say that some people have no doubts about the truth of the story.

The Violation of a Fairy Fort

"Fairy forts" are accorded great respect by most people in all parts of Ireland. A fairy fort can be anything from a 12th-century Anglo-Norman motte (a man-made earthen defensive mound) or a pre-Norman Celtic earthen fort to a Bronze Age stone circle or, especially in Wicklow, an Iron Age rath (a circular earthen bank and ditch surrounding a homestead). Animals can graze on these artefacts, but they cannot be destroyed or ploughed or built on without retribution from the fairies.

In the late 1990s, two woods workers dug into a small rath with a digging machine in a wood near Avoca. Within a few weeks, one of them was killed in a motorcycle accident, and the other, an exceptionally strong man who could pick up a gas cylinder in each hand, was lifting one cylinder to his shoulder when he suffered a massive heart attack and died instantly.

The local man who told me about this did not say the deaths were the result of the violation of the fairy fort, but he put the incidents together in such a way that he obviously felt they were related.

The Moving Statue

On the Vale Road about a quarter-mile south of the White Bridge, there is a statue of the Blessed Virgin erected by the Avoca miners in 1954. One day in September 1986, a couple of schoolgirls saw the statue move. This was at the same time that thousands of people were flocking regularly to the crying statue of the Virgin in Ballinspittle, County Cork. That evening, a light was installed, and crowds gathered and continued to gather for several weeks to watch the statue, plinth and all, appear to bob up and down and back and forth. The local butcher was so strongly affected when he saw it that he took to his bed for a day.

I phoned a report to the news department at RTÉ. When I finished dictating the story, the copy girl asked me if I had seen the statue move. I emphasized the phrase I had used in the report – "I saw it *appear to* move" – as I was and am convinced it was an optical illusion caused by viewing a bright object against a dark, but not black, background, like the planet Venus setting. She asked, "Did you get a fright?" RTÉ sent a television news crew to record the phenomenon. The presenter told me later that he saw the statue appearing to move as soon as he got out of the car, but when he blinked at a certain rate – something about film projector speeds – the effect was cancelled. I suspect he really didn't want to see it move.

I attended frequently to observe various reactions. A homogeneous group – three old men or three young women, for example – would be looking at the statue together. Two would see it move, and the third would not, although he or she might wish to. A lapsed Catholic and his Japanese girlfriend, who were not prepared to believe it possible, saw it move. A visiting German Lutheran friend told me he would convert to Catholicism if it moved for him. He saw it move, but he didn't convert. (See also Miscellaneous Tales: A Mysterious Incident in Rathdangan.)

The Big Snow

The snow started about midnight on the 16th of January 1982 and continued all night and for the next two days and nights, heavy and persistent. On the second morning I only knew it was daylight outside by the clock. The snow had drifted over the door and windows, and it was as dark as night inside. The stack of firewood next to the Waterford stove was quickly depleted. Fortunately, the door opened inwards, and I was able to tunnel through the snow to get to the windfall and deadfall branches I had collected from the Castle Howard woods and stored under the cottage.

By the third morning that wood was also gone, and I tunnelled up to the surface to see where I could find more. It had stopped snowing. From where I lived on the Spink side of the valley across to the Bell Rock, everything had disappeared under a thick white blanket apart from a few sappy, unburnable pine-tree tops. Smoke rose from funnels like ant-holes where the heat of the neighbours' chimneys kept the snow away.

Atop the nearly bare windswept Bell Rock stood a tall long-dead pine – months of fuel – that I had lusted after for years, hoping for a lightning strike to tumble it down to the valley. It was the only source of firewood in sight, so I tied pine branches to my wellies for make-shift snowshoes and set off with my axe and saw down across the railroad track, across the Avoca River and the Vale Road, and up the road around the back of the Bell Rock.

It wasn't long before I had chopped the tree down and sawed off the branches. I reckoned the easiest way to get the wood home was to slide the tree down to the valley, cut it into manageable pieces and haul it up to my cottage bit by bit. I gave it a kick and sent it down the nearly vertical side of the Bell Rock.

It tobogganed down the slope, across the road and the river, but it didn't stop there. The snow was so slippery that it sailed right over the railroad track and up the steep Spink (from the Irish *speanc* = cliff) nearly to the Holy Year Cross. Then down again, across the track, river and road, and back up the Bell Rock. And again down, across, up, down, across, up. I could see what was happening. With each crossing of the valley, the heat caused by the friction of the sliding log melted the snow, which refroze to ice, making the deepening track slipperier.

I went home and had lunch, came back out, and there was the log, still sailing up and down and across. I gave up for the day. The following morning I went out to look for the log and couldn't see it anywhere. I thought someone had stolen the firewood I had worked so hard for. I went down to the river and found a deep trench, and there it was, reduced to the size of a toothpick, still quivering back and forth.

I keep it in my pocket as a reminder of the Big Snow of 1982 ... and to pick my teeth.

Toss Byrne's Stroke

Thomas "Toss" Byrne owned the popular Fountain Pub, now renowned as Fitzgeralds in the TV series *Ballykissangel*. He announced one day that he was going to sell up and move with his family to Canada. He sold the pub for a good price, and his friends and neighbours and customers took up a collection to help them on their way.

But he only went as far as the Woodenbridge Hotel a few miles down the road, which he bought with the proceeds of the sale of the Fountain. All the good will he had built up at the Fountain, along with many of his former customers, relocated along with him. Then he sold the Woodenbridge and bought the pub on the N11 near Gorey in County Wexford still called "Toss Byrne's".

Jimmy Treacy
(1920-2006)

Jimmy was a postman in and around Avoca for 47 years. He always seemed to have time for a few words with the people he met as he putted through his rounds on his motorbike. And he had the ability to make a person feel that the encounter was the high point of Jimmy's day.

After he retired, he recalled, "Some days I'd be sitting in the warm kitchen having my breakfast, and I'd look at the rain lashing against the window and listen to the wind howling around the corners of the house. And I'd say to myself, 'I can't go out in that.' But of course I had to, and you know, I always found that it was never as bad once I got out in it as I thought it would be."

Miscellaneous Tales

A Redcross Púca

In 1959, Dermot Mac Manus published a collection of anecdotes called *The Middle Kingdom* about modern encounters with denizens of the world of faerie. The stories were told to him, with a few exceptions, by people to whom the incidents happened and whom he knew personally. "A Wicklow Pooka" (Irish *púca*) begins typically: "In 1952 a friend of mine, Margo Ryan, a charming and intelligent girl, encountered the Pooka ..."

The story takes place near Redcross, which is about four miles up the hill northeast of Avoca and not far from Pollaphuca (Pool of the Púca), a common place-name throughout Ireland. Margo was walking near her home late one Midsummer evening, when there was still some light in the sky. She heard a patter of feet and turned to see a large black dog walking next to her. She tried several times to touch it, but her hand went right through it, even though it looked solid. It walked beside her for a few minutes, then suddenly vanished.

"Let there be no doubt about it whatever," Mac Manus emphasises, "it did not run off but actually vanished from where it stood in the centre of the road." To counter the obvious explanation, he points out that country people know what a Labrador looks like, and púcas are not Labradors; similar, but considerably larger. I would add that country people are also well acquainted with the dogs of their neighbours.

Poulaphuca

Some years ago, I asked a waitress at the Poulaphuca Inn near Blessington if she knew the story of how the pool under the waterfall, part of the course of the River Liffey, behind the hotel came to be named the Pool of the Púca. She made up a yarn on the spot about a púca being knocked down by a car, probably inspired by the fact that a lorry had recently crashed through the parapet of the bridge over the waterfall. I asked her if she knew the real story, and she admitted that she didn't. Here it is, paraphrased from Padraic O'Farrell's *Irish Ghost Stories*.

In 1813, before the bridge was built, the Kildare Hunt was chasing a fox, when a large black riderless horse joined them as they neared the waterfall. The fox leapt across the gorge but failed to get a grip on the opposite ledge and fell into the pool. The horse made the jump successfully, and the hounds attempted to follow it but fell into the pool. The fox managed to swim to safety, but most of the hounds were lost.

Most púcas reported in the Republic are large black dogs with fiery red eyes (see The Vale of Avoca: The Avoca Púca), but some, as in this case, take the form of horses.

The Ball Moat

A few steps down a lane off the square of Donard village and next to Moat Farm and the ruins of a 15th- or 16th-century church and graveyard is an Anglo-Norman motte, a man-made defensive mound possibly built by Jordan de Marisco about 1190. ("Moat" and "mote" are frequent local spellings and pronunciations of "motte".) It is about sixty feet in diameter and twenty feet high with a six-foot depression in the top caused by treasure hunters, the sort of depression found in many mottes. Stories similar to this are told about other mottes and burial sites.

In the *Journal of the Royal Society of Antiquaries of Ireland* (1931),[115] Patrick T. Walshe wrote that Mr Allen of Donard told him that

> a Mr. Cardel, who died many years ago in Donard, related to him that there was always a local belief that gold was hidden in this mound. It was ultimately decided by a number of residents to excavate it, but according to tradition these residents dared not begin their work till "a life was taken" on the spot where they were about to dig. Accordingly they took a cock with them to the summit and killed it there.
>
> They then began to work, but after proceeding to the depth above indicated a "black bull" leaped forth from the opening and the assembled people fled in terror.

A sceptic to whom I told this tale dismissed it as "a cock and bull story".

"Ned Sheehy of Dromin"

This is a story told by one of "O'Dwyer's" (Michael Dwyer's) men in the cottage at Derrynamuck as they are bedding down for the night, in Gerald Griffin's semi-fictional account of the Dwyer-McAllister incident, "Antrim Jack, and His General".[116] I have edited it slightly for clarity.

> "Why, he was known for a notorious night-walker, and like our general here, they were looking for him night and day for months, and could never catch him. At last they put a few lines in the paper to say

---

[115] Walshe, p. 123.
[116] Griffin, *Talis Qualis*, p. 367.

that if the nearest relation of the late Jerry Sheehy, a cousin of his that wasn't dead at all, would come to some office in Dublin, he'd hear something to his advantage. Poor Ned was always very covetous for money, so he went there, and they pinned him. When he axed 'em what he had to learn to his advantage, they told him he ought to have been hanged long ago, but they'd only transport him for life."

A Mysterious Incident in Rathdangan

Autumn of 1986 was the season of the moving statues in Ireland, beginning with the crying statue of the Blessed Virgin in Ballinspittle in County Cork. (See also The Vale of Avoca: The Moving Statue.) Most statues are painted in more or less natural colours and stand lighted against a dark but not black background. This can give the illusion of movement. The one in Rathdangan is painted now, but at that time it was completely white. It stood alone in stark contrast to the black sky at night.

The statue was lighted, and a fair-sized crowd would gather every evening to spend hours staring at the statue and praying the rosary. No one reported seeing that statue move, but they said the facial features changed constantly to resemble Christ, Padre Pio, Saint Joseph and others.

I went there only once, but a friend of mine attended frequently, and she told me this story. A teenaged boy was standing on the bank of the ditch opposite the statue one evening, mocking the crowd for their belief. Suddenly, he was pushed off the bank from behind. When he discovered that no one had been behind him, he became hysterical and ran down the road so fast his friends had to get into a car to catch him.

The Gates of Heaven, Kilranelagh Cemetery
(front cover photo)

For those not wealthy enough to avail of the shortcut to Paradise by being buried in Reefert, Saint Kevin's Royal Cemetery in Glendalough (page 14), it is a local custom to carry a coffin between these two stones so that the deceased will go straight to heaven. They have been variously identified as the remaining orthostats of a prehistoric tomb and the surviving gateposts of an earlier graveyard. Aedh Ainmire, the 6-century High King who lost the Battle of Dún Bolg and his head in the Bórama saga, is believed to be buried in this cemetery. Sam McAllister (see Michael Dwyer chapter), Dwyer's sister Mary, and John Moore (see The Hanging of John Moore chapter) also rest here. The largely neglected graveyard is next to the ruins of the 14th-century Kilranelagh Church, dedicated to Saint Brigit, on Kilranelagh Hill near Baltinglass.

Saint Bridget's Head Stone

At the base of the northwest corner of Kilranelagh Hill near Baltinglass is a semi-perforated worked round stone about five feet in diameter. A perfectly round hole has been bored partway through the centre, and it looks like a broken millstone. It is called Saint Bridget's Head Stone – *Clogh na gCeann* in Irish, literally "Stone of the Head". The townland in which it is located, Cloghnagaune, takes its name from the stone. Saint Brigit is now mainly associated with Kildare, but historically East Kildare and West Wicklow are essentially the same territory. There are two explanations for the name "Head Stone".

Local people place their heads into the hole to cure headaches, especially chronic headaches for which orthodox medicine has proved ineffective. In payment they leave coins, rosaries, religious medals and prayer cards in the hole and on the branches of the overhanging hazel tree. I took a Spanish friend, Elvira, to the Stone, but before I could explain what it was for she had put her head into the hole. She didn't have a headache before, but she had one afterwards. I took an Irish friend to the Stone, but before I could tell her how it worked, she had put her head into the hole. She had had a headache before, but it went away immediately that she put her head into the hole.

The other explanation is that either Cummascach or Aedh Ainmire or both had their heads chopped off on the stone in the Bórama saga.

Baltinglass Bell Tower

"Before Catholic emancipation, it was illegal to summon a Catholic congregation by a bell from a Roman Catholic church or chapel." So the Reverend John Shea built the square tower that still stands north of the old burial ground in the grounds of the Catholic church on Chapel Hill in Baltinglass, and the bell was rung from there. As this observed the letter of the law, the authorities were unable to prevent this clever circumvention of its spirit.[117]

Shawn Reilly

In Baltinglass during the 1798 Rebellion, "one Shawn Reilly was closely pursued by the military. He was seen to enter a gateway that leads to several houses. Reilly made for one, in which churning was going on, and was clapped into the churn. The soldiers, having searched the other houses,

---

[117] O'Kelly, pp. 337-8.

entered this, but the churning proceeded. A servant, named Maggie Doyle, who had been jilted by Reilly, got a kettle of boiling water and commenced to scald the churn. Poor Reilly couldn't cry out, but as soon as the soldiers disappeared he was speedily released." [118]

The Athgreany Stone Circle

South of Hollywood next to the N81 and well signposted, this well-preserved stone circle has a simple story. People dancing on a Sunday were turned to stone for their irreverence, the outlier (a stone lying outside the circle) being the piper. The outlier and the entrance stones are in a direct line with the setting sun at the Midwinter Solstice. "Athgreany" is the Anglicised *Achadh Gréinne*, "Field of the Sun". Inside the circle, the fallen but vigorously growing whitethorn fairy tree is often bedecked with gifts for the resident spirits.

"The Night We Riz the Tan"

Early in 1920, during the War of Independence, Thomas Frederick Aikens shot himself in the RIC (Royal Irish Constabulary) barracks in Hollywood and was buried in the Catholic section of the Protestant cemetery there. Why a Protestant – presumably, judging by his name – was buried with the Catholics is not known: possibly because the Protestants didn't want a suicide among their dead. Local memory is vague on whether Aikens was an RIC man or a member of the Black and Tans, the ex-army irregulars recruited as an auxiliary to the RIC and notorious for their brutality.

In any case, he was buried on a Saturday, and that night three local IRA men "riz" the coffin and set it upright outside the cemetery with a note attached: "The will of the people – bury him elsewhere." People on their way to Mass or services the following morning were shocked at the sight, and not many would have agreed that the action reflected their will.

The local undertaker took the coffin to the military cemetery at the Curragh for interment.

Over the years, "the night we [or they] riz the Tan" lost nothing in the re-telling, especially by one of the long-lived participants. For example, Aikens came to be credited with occult powers – he could move things invisibly and make his blackthorn stick dance – and he was possessed.

John Glennon, whose book-in-progress "The History of Hollywood" is my source for this incident, ends his account with: "For the people of Hollywood looking back the Black and Tan War was encapsulated in that

---

[118] O'Kelly, p. 337.

eerie night and shocking morning." He told me, "If you mention the Troubles, it's the one thing the people will tell you."

That's the tale as remembered by the people of Hollywood. At the suggestion of Henry Cairns of the Townhall Bookshop in Bray, I consulted Richard Abbott's *Police Casualties in Ireland 1919-1921* (Mercier 2000) to see if there was any documentary evidence to support the story. "Thomas Frederick Aikens" is not listed. The nearest entry is: "[RIC number] 76402 Ikin ['Ilkin' in the index] Thomas F. Constable 08.08.1921. Suicide." No location or other details are given. John Glennon reckons this is Aikens.

A Bray Ghost Story

After the artistic community broke up, a youngish couple with children bought Tigroney House. (See The Vale of Avoca: The Tigroney Ghost.) I asked them if they knew about the ghost. They didn't. The woman was enthusiastic, but the man said he didn't believe in ghosts and was adamant that he didn't want to hear about it. The woman persisted, and when I finished the story, she told me about the haunted house they had lived in in Bray.

When they were in the sitting room watching television one evening, they heard heavy adult footsteps coming down the stairs, which were just the other side of the wall against which the couch was set. The door to the hall was next to the couch, and it didn't take two seconds to stand up and turn and open the door to look into the hall and up the stairs. No one was on the stairs or in the hall, and the children were in bed and asleep. This happened frequently, and although the man – a construction engineer – insisted that he did not believe in ghosts, he had to admit that he heard footsteps that had no physical explanation.

Saint Patrick in Wicklow

Saint Patrick was captured in a raid on Britain led by High King Niall of the Nine Hostages and brought to Ireland as a slave. He escaped after ten years, became a bishop, and returned to Ireland in AD 432, according to popular tradition.

In Arklow, they say he landed there. The fresh water had run out on the boat. Patrick was the first to step ashore, and where his foot fell a well sprang up. Modern historians dismiss this story as medieval political propaganda.

Residents of Wicklow Town and others who don't hold with Patrick's first landfall as bishop being Arklow say he landed in Wicklow. This claim is supported by long-standing tradition, ancient records and the fact that the

"Pudeen", Patrick's Little Rock, was installed at the back of the East Pier as witness to the event.

Unfortunately for Patrick, his predecessor, Palladius, had landed in Wicklow Town the previous year. The local chief was Náth Í Mac Garrchon, who was married to the daughter of High King Laeghaire, son of Niall of the Nine Hostages. Náth Í and his people had thrown stones at Palladius and made him feel unwelcome enough that he went off to found churches in Avoca, Donard and at Killeen Cormac near Dunlavin.

So when Patrick arrived in Wicklow Town, the residents said, "Here's more of those Christians. There goes the neighbourhood." And they pelted Patrick and his entourage with stones. They missed Patrick but hit one of his followers and knocked out his teeth. The man was dubbed "Mantán", which means Toothless, and that is how Wicklow County and Town got their Irish name: Cill Mhantáin – the Church of Mantán.

As a result, Patrick placed a curse on the town that the makings of a priest would never come from there.

A Rathnew Stroke

A poor widow living in a cottage in Rathnew fell into arrears in her rent, and after several warnings the bailiffs arrived to evict her. As soon as they had moved all her furniture into the front garden, she suddenly produced the full of the back rent.

"Why didn't you pay the rent before we went to all the trouble of moving this furniture out?" they asked in amazement.

"Never mind that," she said. "Ye can go now and have your lunch, and then come back and put all the furniture back where it was."

They went away, and while they were gone the widow gave the cottage the first thorough cleaning it had had in years, which of course was the reason she wanted the furniture temporarily removed at no cost to herself.

(Rathnew was founded in 125 BC by Nui, brother of Nuada Necht, 45th king of Ireland.)

The Glenmalure Man

This is how I remember a story that appeared in *The Wicklow People* some time in the 1980s.

A Jew, a Hindu and a man from Glenmalure were hill-walking somewhere on the Continent, found themselves lost at nightfall, and sought accommodation at a farmhouse. They knocked on the door, the farmer opened it, and they explained their predicament.

"Sure, you're welcome to spend the night, but the problem is we have beds for only two of ye. One of ye will have to sleep in the barn."

"No problem," said the Jew. "I'll sleep in the barn." Off he went. The other two tucked themselves into the spare beds and the household had just settled down to sleep when there was a knock on the door. It was the Jew.

"I'm sorry to bother you, but there's a pig in the barn, and as I'm a Jew and pig meat is forbidden to us ..."

"No problem," said the Hindu. "I'll sleep in the barn." Off he toddled. The other two tucked themselves into bed and the household settled down to sleep. There was a knock on the door. It was the Hindu.

"I'm sorry to bother you, but there's a cow in the barn, and as I'm a Hindu and cows are sacred to us ..."

"No problem," said the Glenmalure man. "I'll sleep in the barn." Off he went. No sooner had the household settled down to sleep than there was a knock on the door.

It was the pig and the cow.

Notes on the Stories

The Naming of Baltinglass

Belach Dubhtaire

Dubhtaire means "jungle", which aptly describes the heavily forested Baltinglass district before the Cistercians cleared the land for farming in the 12th century. Shearman derives *dubhtaire* from "Dubthaire, son of Fergna, King of the Deisi Breg" in County Meath, and applies the name to the waterfall at Poulaphuca (see Miscellaneous Tales: Poulaphuca), between Blessington and Hollywood, which Glas passed in the chase – "Aes Dubthaire, i.e. the Cataract of Dubthaire, who also gave his name to Beallach Dubthaire, the oldest name of the pass or road at Baltinglass".[119] The atmospheric ravine into which the now-reduced cataract trickles is heavily wooded. The waterfall is on the Kildare side of the zigzagging county border.

The Melodies of Buchet's House

Buchet

Although this story is a straightforward tale in the form in which it has come down to us from the 10th century, a mystique ranging from the magical to the mythic surrounds the character of Buchet. Some folklorists see him as a humanised fertility god ("ultimately he represents the Otherworld-deity"),[120] citing the epithet "cauldron of hospitality" (*coire féile*) as evidence that he is an aspect of the Dagda Mór. Buchet and his wife figure in the 1st-century BC story of the demon Swine of Drebrenn, who are central to the chase that resulted in The Naming of Baltinglass, and Buchet's House figures in the Bórama saga. A lost tale called "Feis Dúin Buchet" is mentioned in a tale-list in the *Book of Leinster*.

Buchet's House and Dún Buchet

"Buchet's House" is the direct translation of *tech in Buichet* in this story. The site of Saint Kevin's church at Dunboyke near Hollywood is said by some to have been the site of Buchet's House, because Dunboyke seems to derive from *Dún Buchet*, as Buchet's House is called in some stories. O'Rahilly says this "is no more than a bad guess. The Irish name of

---

[119] Shearman, pp. 28-9.
[120] O'Rahilly, p. 12.

Dunboyke is Dún Búacci." [121] Price believed that Buchet's House was "at or near the present Kilranelagh House" on Kilranelagh Hill.[122]

"Ranelagh" probably comes from *ranarech*, a later form of *(h)erenach*. (The "Ranelagh" derived from Feagh McHugh O'Byrne's sept Gabhal Raghnaill and applied to their territory, while geographically close, is not etymologically related.) A *herenach* or *rannaire* was a dispenser of church property but also "one who divides and distributes solid food, esp. meat, at meals" (DIL). *Rannaid* is used with a sense of the dispensing of hospitality by innkeepers (DIL). This close association of the hospitaller Buchet with a place that retains *rannaire* in its name seriously weakens the argument for siting Dún Buchet or Buchet's House at Dunboyke, and supports the setting at Kilranelagh.

Saint Kevin and Glendalough

The Water Monster

Stories of the *each uisce* – "water horse" – are attached to many lakes and rivers in Ireland. According to Samuel Lover: "Eels of uncommon size are said to exist in the upper lake of Glendalough: the guides invariably tell marvellous stories of them: they describe them of forbidding aspect, with manes as large as a horse's; – one of these 'slippery rogues' is said to have amused himself by entering a pasture on the borders of the lake, and eating a cow – maybe 'twas a bull." [123]

Kevin and Fáelán

Liam Price said: "The story sounds as if it had a historical basis; it would be natural enough for the king to send his son to the monastery in fosterage to a member of a royal race of Leinster, a race which was, however, no longer a rival to Colman's own family, the Ui Dunluing, for the kingship; and there is nothing far-fetched in supposing that the stepmother would ally herself with the priests of the old religion for the purpose of removing her stepson, who was being brought up in the new Christian faith." [124]

---

[121] O'Rahilly, p. 8n.

[122] Price, *Place-names*, p. 121.

[123] Lover, *Legends and Stories*, p. 14 note.

[124] Price, *Place-names*, p. 4, where he recounts a slightly different version of the story.

Kevin's Bed

Modern-day hikers who venture into Kevin's Bed (Glendalough) frequently have to be rescued by helicopter when they find themselves unable to descend or ascend. A writer for the *Dublin Penny Journal* described the cave as "not bigger than a small baker's oven ... I, and two young men who followed me, found it a very tight fit when crouched together in it".[125] Sir Walter Scott (1771-1832) entered the cave in July 1825. His son-in-law, J. G. Lockhart, wrote to his wife:

> It is a hole in the sheer surface of the rock, in which two or three people might sit. The difficulty of getting into this place is exaggerated, as also the danger, for it would only be falling thirty or forty feet into very deep water. Yet I was never more pained than when your papa, in spite of all remonstrances, would make his way to it, crawling along the precipice. He succeeded and got in – the first lame man that ever tried it.[126]

Kevin and Cathleen

Distinct from Lover's song but obviously owing much to it, "The Glendalough Saint" – "Words and Music: Traditional (Midlands)" – in James N. Healy's 1962 *The Second Book of Irish Ballads* is essentially the same as Dominic Behan's "The Saint" (with "new words and music by Dominic Behan from the singing of [his father] Stephen Behan") in his 1973 *Ireland Sings*. A note in Behan's book says: "My father has about two versions of this song ... The other version he only sings to shock the company."

Allowing for the workings of the folk process, that is the song most people know from the singing of Ronnie Drew of The Dubliners.

Fingal Rónáin

This is an early 10th-century literary fiction preserved in the 12th-century *Book of Leinster*. In the muddled outline form in which it appears in the 17th-century *Annals of Ireland* at Eochaid Iarlaithe's death date of 664, it seems meant to be taken as fact. The "torn head scarf and scratched and bleeding face" element is found only in the *Annals of Ireland*. I have based my version on Kuno Meyer's edition and translation in *Revue Celtique* 13, 1892, with the aid of David Greene's edition and notes in *Fingal Rónáin*.

---

[125] *Dublin Penny Journal*, Vol. III, No. 123, Nov 8, 1834, p. 151.
[126] Lockhart, p. 559.

Direct quotes from Meyer are indicated. I have inserted a few sentences for narrative flow.

The fictional Rónán mac Aed is based partly on at least one of the two 7th-century historical kings of Leinster named Rónán mac Colmáin, one of whom died in AD 610 or 624 "of a running of blood" (*de rith fola*). Elizabeth Gabay, a medical doctor in the United States, has given me this interpretation of the description of Rónán's death:

> "A rush of blood" immediately preceding death sounds like a haemorrhage from the upper digestive system, such as bleeding from a stomach or duodenal ulcer. The stress Rónán was under at the time suggests this. However, the quickest and most dramatic such death would occur from rupture of a varix (a dilated vein along the oesophagus caused by alcoholic liver disease.) The liver disease increases the pressure in the veins and they swell up; a very bad liver also affects the blood so that it doesn't clot normally. A person can bleed massively from the mouth and die within a few minutes. Another way to die suddenly from bleeding from the mouth is erosion of a lung cancer into an artery. These modes of death are uncommon in modern times but were probably frequent hundreds of years ago.

Rónán mac Colmáin was the brother or half-brother of Saint Kevin's foster son Fáelán. But there was a historical Uí Máil king of Leinster named Rónán mac Aed who was also guilty of a kin-slaying (*fingal*). He killed his brother, the king, in 633 so that he could be king. This Rónán's grandson Fiannamail was killed in a battle at Bae Aife (also called Selg) in 680. Two of his great-grandsons were killed in another battle at Bae Aife in 709. The name "Mael Fhothartaig" does not appear historically in Leinster at this time.

Rónán's royal seat, Ráth Imáil, may be Crossoona Rath, a ringfort on Kilranelagh Hill not far from Bae Aife. Michael Dwyer used Crossoona Rath during a running skirmish in early September 1798.

Feagh McHugh O'Byrne

Background

1553-8. Henry VIII's half-Spanish Catholic daughter, Mary I (Mary Tudor), is queen, marries her cousin Philip II of Spain. Under "Bloody Mary", the Counter-Reformation claims over 300 Protestant martyrs.

1558. Elizabeth becomes queen on Mary's death and re-establishes Protestantism.

1570. Pope Pius V excommunicates Queen Elizabeth.

1577. At least 180 Leinster chiefs and members of their families are massacred after they were invited to meet, under safe conduct, with government officers for a parlay at the Rath of Mullaghmast in County Kildare.

In the Rath of Mullaghmast,
That dreadful day is passed,
When the Tories called us in for protection,
Their slaughter they began,
And they killed us every man,
Left our widows and poor orphans there crying.
from "The Ancient Memory of Mullaghmast in the County of Kildare"
– Anon [127]

1580, July. Letters published in Waterford assert that the Pope, the King of Spain and the Duke of Florence have leagued together to provide 33,000 infantry and 2660 cavalry to the Irish.[128]

1580, October-November. Some 600 Italian troops sent to Ireland by the Pope, with the aid of Spain, in support of Irish Catholics are quickly overwhelmed by the English, surrender, and are summarily executed on orders of Lord Deputy Grey.

1585. Open conflict with Spain. England is nervous – with good reason – that Spain will use Ireland as a back door to attack England.

1588. The Spanish Armada begins Spain's Fifteen Years' War with England. Of 130 ships that sailed, 63 are lost, with about 20 wrecked on Irish coasts. Three thousand survivors who land in Ireland are massacred [129] – over 1100 in Connacht alone – on orders of Lord Deputy Fitzwilliam.

1591. Red Hugh O'Donnell escapes from Dublin Castle with the aid of Feagh McHugh O'Byrne. Ulster Catholic bishops work in the background for rebellion.

1592. The fulfilment of a prophecy – when one Hugh O'Donnell succeeds another, he will banish the conquerors and become king of Ireland[130] – is anticipated when Red Hugh, aged 19, succeeds his father, Hugh Manus, as O'Donnell chief.

When two Hughs, the Black and the Red,
Lawfully and lineally follow each other as O'Donnell,
The latter shall be Ard Rí
And banish the Stranger.[131]

---

[127] Madden, *Literary Remains*, p. 171.
[128] Cox, the second of two pages numbered "367".
[129] *Calendar of the Carew Manuscripts,* Vol. 2, p. 471 – letter from Sir George Carew to Sir Francis Walsingham 18 September 1588.
[130] Ó hÓgáin, p. 337.
[131] "Old Donegal ballad", Faolain, p. 89.

1593. Ulster chiefs and bishops appeal to Philip II for a crusade to liberate Ireland "from the rod of tyrannical evil" and "ministers of satanic fury".[132]

1594. Nine Years' War begins with the rising of Red Hugh O'Donnell.

1595. Hugh O'Neill, Earl of Tyrone, joins the rising.

1596. Hugh O'Neill recognises Philip III of Spain as king of Ireland. Spain promises aid to Irish Catholics.

1596, September. Feagh McHugh rises in anticipation of a successful landing of Spanish troops.

1596, October. Spain launches its disastrous "Second Armada", which is immediately destroyed.

1597, May 8. Feagh is betrayed and killed.

"Follow Me Up to Carlow"

Marching Song of Feagh MacHugh.

"The Firebrand of the Mountains"

A.D. 1580.

It is a tradition that this air ("Follow me up to Carlow") was first performed by the pipers of Feagh MacHugh as he marched to attack Carlow after his victory over Lord Deputy Grey at Glenmalure. MacCahir Ogue was Brian MacCahir Cavanagh, whom Fitzwilliam had driven out of his possessions.

> Lift, MacCahir Ogue, your face,
> Brooding o'er the old disgrace,
> That black Fitzwilliam stormed your place,
>   And drove you to the fern!
> Grey said victory was sure –
> Soon The Firebrand he'd secure;
> Until he met at Glenmalure,
>   Feagh MacHugh O'Byrne!
>
>   Chaunt –
> Curse and swear, Lord Kildare!
> Feagh will do what Feagh will dare –
> Now, Fitzwilliam, have a care –

---

[132] Falls, p. 195.

Fallen is your star, low!
Up with halbert, out with sword!
On we go; for, by the Lord!
Feagh MacHugh has given the word –
Follow me up to Carlow!

See the swords of Glen Imayle
Flashing o'er the English Pale!
See all the children of the Gael
        Beneath O'Byrne's banners!
Rooster of a fighting stock,
Would you let a Saxon cock
Crow out upon an Irish rock?
        Fly up, and teach him manners!

Chaunt –
Curse and swear, Lord Kildare! etc.

From Tassagart to Clonmore
Flows a stream of Saxon gore!
Och, great is Rory Ogue O'More
        At sending loons to Hades!
White is sick, and Lane is fled!
Now for black Fitzwilliam's head –
We'll send it over dripping red
        To 'Liza* and her ladies!

Chaunt –
Curse and swear, Lord Kildare! etc.

* Queen Elizabeth.

The above is reproduced as it appears in the 1899 collection *Songs of Erinn*, by Patrick Joseph McCall (1861-1919). Feagh and other O'Byrnes frequently attacked Carlow. No specific attack at this time has attracted the attention of the historians.

"MacCahir Ogue" is Brian McCahir Kavanagh. His father, Cahir McArt Kavanagh, led a revolt in 1548. Brian was married to Feagh's sister Elizabeth. Based in the barony of Saint Mullins (the monastery founded by Saint Mo Ling of the Bórama saga), he was involved in the Butler/Kavanagh revolt in 1569 on the side of Irish and "Old English" (Anglo-Irish) landowners against the "New English" (English-born newcomers). "And drove you to the fern" suggests he was driven into the hills when his home was stormed. A variant text has "the Ferns", which may relate to the unsubstantiated allegation that Feagh McHugh and Brian McCahir Kavanagh burned Ferns Abbey and Castle in Wexford in the summer of 1577. See also "White" below.

"Fitzwilliam" – Sir William Fitzwilliam, Lord Deputy 1571-75 and 1588-1594: "a capable and conscientious ruler", according to one modern English historian,[133] but his name is blackened by early historians for profiting from his office. Some English writers have strongly implied that his maladministration *caused* the Nine Years' War. He is suspected of having accepted a bribe – among many – to facilitate the escape of Red Hugh O'Donnell from Dublin Castle in 1591.[134] He was directly responsible for the slaughter of shipwrecked Armada survivors.

"Grey" – See Feagh McHugh O'Byrne chapter.

"Lord Kildare" – The "Old English" Fitzgeralds of Kildare were Lords Deputy from the late 15th century through the reign of Henry VIII, and generally loyal to the Crown and a powerful influence afterwards. It was said of the Kildare who was Lord Deputy in 1510 that "his Name was more terrible to the Irish than an Army",[135] but in 1467 the Earl of Kildare had been convicted of "high treason, for having formed alliance with the Irish enemy, and supporting him against the king, by supplying him with arms and horses, in contempt of the laws of the prince and the statutes of the realm".[136] The family motto is: "*De Geraldinis fertur ipsis Hibernicis Hiberniores fuisse* – The Geraldines are said to be more Irish than the Irish themselves."

"Halbert" (usually "halberd") – This is the mis-named "pike" of the 1798 Rebellion. A pike was up to 16 feet in length, used by pikemen to protect musketeers against a cavalry charge while they reloaded. A halberd was "a modified pike with an axehead, a weapon that could be used for cutting or smashing as well as thrusting".[137] "The halberd was one of the most versatile pole-arms of the fifteenth and sixteenth centuries. It could be used to hook an enemy to the ground, even if he was on horseback, as well as for chopping and thrusting." [138]

"Tassagart / Clonmore" – Tasaggart is an old place-name around the modern village of Saggart (from *Teach an tSagairt* – "house of the priest") in southwest County Dublin, which was in the Pale. It is recorded as having

---

[133] Falls, p. 183.

[134] Morgan, pp. 131-33; Cox, p. 400; O'Grady, *Captivity*, p. 162; et al.

[135] Cox, p. 200.

[136] O'Byrne, *Historical Reminiscences*, p. 18.

[137] Edwards, p. 242.

[138] Harding, p. 57.

been burned by O'Byrnes and O'Tooles in 1471 and was a frequent target. The rebels attacked it in September 1580. Clonmore is in Carlow just over the Wicklow border. Its prominent monastery was first raided by Vikings in 836, and the town was attacked by rebels in all periods. The author of "Follow Me Up to Carlow", P. J. McCall, is buried there.

"Rory Ogue O'More", "that indefatigable Rebel",[139] was chief of the O'Mores of Leix (modern Laois). He was an ally of Hugh McShane and was married to Feagh's sister Margaret, who was killed by the English in 1577. In 1556, under Queen Mary, Leix was singled out for intensive planting of English settlers. Rory "gave trouble" in 1572 and was killed in 1578. Some histories of the period give him more space than Feagh. At least 40 O'Mores were killed in the 1577 Mullaghmast massacre. (See Feagh McHugh O'Byrne: Background, 1577.) Rory's son, Owen McRory O'More, who was raised by Feagh McHugh, became a rebel commander as soon as he came of age about 1597. The ancestry of the poet Thomas Moore is traced from these O'Mores.

"White" is Nicholas White, Seneschal of Wexford, who in May 1572 accused Feagh McHugh and Brian McCahir Kavanagh of the murder of his daughter's husband, Robert Browne of Mulrankin, near Wexford. White rashly stated publicly that the Queen would never pardon anyone connected with the murder, and then he attacked O'Byrne territory in South Wicklow. This forced Feagh and Brian into open revolt. They were pardoned 15 February 1573.

"Lane" – Sir Ralph Lane was muster-master general of Ireland at this time. Some versions of the song substitute the more recognisable "Grey" for "Lane".

Michael Dwyer

State Terrorism

Pitch-capping was the practice of fixing a cap of melted pitch (tar) to a person's head, or mixing grease and gunpowder in his hair, and setting it alight. Picketing involved suspending a prisoner with his foot resting on a sharpened stake, and rotating him. Half-hanging meant repeatedly hanging a prisoner short of killing him. Those were methods used during interrogations to obtain information about insurgents. Raking a prisoner's face or legs with spurs and tying his arms to the saddles of two running horses seem to have been merely for amusement.

---

[139] Cox, p. 354.

Because of a shortage of prison space, many able-bodied prisoners were sold as slaves to the King of Prussia to work in the mines.

The number of churches burned does not necessarily reflect the number of church-burnings. Mrs O'Toole said the church at Maccredan near Aughrim was burned three times.

"The country was proclaimed."

One such proclamation was a resolution passed by the Wicklow Magistracy 3 April 1798, quoted in full in Cullen (pp. 153-5), which says in part: "... proclaiming the county to be in a state of disturbance ... In no point are the rights of the peaceful and honest man infringed" by "this act of necessary severity". Surrendering arms and "refraining from seditious meetings" will "restore you again to the full enjoyment of that glorious and inimitable constitution which has rendered these kingdoms the admiration of the world".

Description and Character of Dwyer

A contemporary magazine article gave Dwyer's height as 5 feet, 7 inches. His brother, Hugh, said he was 5-11½. Dwyer lost his left thumb in a firearm accident in the summer of 1803: he fired off his blunderbuss in frustration at not being able to catch up with an informer before he reached Dublin. Several people living in South Wicklow have told me that Dwyer is not well liked in the area, without being able to specify a reason. One woman, spelling out the word in the presence of her two-year-old granddaughter, said, "He is considered a right b-a-s-t-a-r-d."

The Dwyer-McAllister Incident

The account I give above is compiled from a variety of sources. The story is well documented in several versions, all in substantial agreement. (One variant has ten men altogether in two cottages; one source calls the location "Bernamuck", which is not recorded as a place-name in Wicklow, another "Barnamuck", a local variant of Derrynamuck.) It is the most widely disseminated story about Dwyer, appearing in scholarly, oral history and semi-fictional accounts.

A lively version, "Antrim Jack, and His General", is included in *Talis Qualis*, the 1842 posthumous short story collection by the prominent 19th-century poet and prose writer Gerald Griffin. In the story, the noticeably effeminate McAllister figure, Antrim Jack, has a strong emotional attachment to "O'Dwyer" (the Michael Dwyer character) – usually sleeping by his side – that suggests a homosexual attraction. Antrim Jack, like McAllister, is from Antrim and is called "Antrim Jack" because, Griffin said, "the name of this person we cannot at present call to mind". Griffin, who died in 1840, was writing when many of McAllister's immediate family and friends were still alive, and he may have been wary of giving offence or being sued for libel. Griffin is probably the source – I've found no other – of statements by later writers that "Antrim Jack" was McAllister's nickname.

An "Antrim Jack" Dogherty was killed in a battle in November 1798 at Ballyfad near Coolgreany, and his head was displayed on a pike in Gorey or Arklow or both. At least three "Antrim Johns" deserted from the Antrim Militia and fought with the rebels in Wicklow and Wexford.

Griffin inserts a short yarn (see Miscellaneous Tales: "Ned Sheehy of Dromin") told while the men are bedding down for the night, and after building up Antrim Jack as a brave and conscientious person, gives him a dramatic entrance for his death scene. "O'Dwyer" and Antrim Jack have been discussing life and death for four closely printed pages after "the conflagration had now reached its full strength".

At this instant the door was flung wide, and the appalling figure of Antrim Jack, black, burning, and hideous, appeared amid a volume of smoke and cinders, for a moment before them [the soldiers]. There was an air of excitement about him; a strange, wild kind of light in his eyes, and an expression of pleasure on his half destroyed face.[140]

A colour print of McAllister's death and Dwyer's escape from the cottage is among many articles, pictures and summaries of the careers of Dwyer, Feagh McHugh O'Byrne and other historical figures of local interest on display in pubs in the area, including the Michael Dwyer Bar and Lounge at Drumgoff crossroads in Glenmalure.

A statue of a man with a musket stands prominently in the Triangle in Baltinglass. It was vandalised shortly after it was erected because of local bad feeling about Dwyer. The inscription reads:

To Commemorate
the
Heroism and Sacrifices
of
Michael Dwyer
and
His Faithful Comrade
Sam MacAllister,
and also
To Perpetuate the Memory
of those who participated
in the

---

[140] Griffin, *Talis Qualis*, p. 380.

Insurrectionary Movements
of
1798, 1803, 1848 and 1867
This Monument has been
Erected by the People of Wicklow County
God Save Ireland
1904

The Irish government bought the "Dwyer-McAllister" cottage and restored it as a museum in 1948. The National Monuments Department of the Office of Public Works maintains it and keeps it open free of charge to the public during the summer. It is signposted generously in the area.

The Dunlavin Green Massacre

Dwyer knew or was related to many of the nearly fifty United Irishmen prisoners massacred in Dunlavin by the Ancient Britons on 24 May 1798. An uncle, John Dwyer, was among them. The numbers of victims usually given for the "Dunlavin Green" massacre are 36 shot en masse on the Green, of whom one survived, and four hanged in the jail (now the library and courtroom). But Chris Lawlor, author of *The Massacre on Dunlavin Green*, has pointed out that the total number killed should be revised to at least the mid-forties (Lawlor, "Dunlavin Green Revisited"). This event eclipsed the murder of twelve prisoners by the Ancient Britons in similar circumstances in the nearby town of Ballymore-Eustace on the same day.

The Military Roads

Both Dwyer and the government must have been familiar with the identical tactic advised by Edmund Spenser in 1596 to capture the elusive Feagh McHugh O'Byrne of Glenmalure. The plan was used successfully to trap and kill Feagh in 1597. The Rathfarnham-Aghavannagh road was built 1800-09, the Glencree-Sally Gap-Laragh road in 1802-04. Contracts were awarded in March 1803 to build five barracks in Dwyer's theatre of operation: in the Glens of Imaal and Glenmalure and at Laragh, Aghavannagh and Glencree. There was also a proposal to have Highlanders and Fencibles (troops licensed to fight outside Britain) build military roads and then settle on free homesteads along the roads to secure them against insurgents. Apparently the troops, aware of the poor quality of the land, wanted no part of the scheme.

The Outlaw's Bridal

This is the first stanza of fifteen of a romantic account by John Thomas Campion of Michael and Mary Dwyer's wedding.[141]

> As the torrent bounds down from the mountain
> Of cloud-helmed stormy Kaigeen,
> And tosses, all tawny and foaming
> Through the still glen of lone Carrageen;[142]
> So dashed a bold rider of Wicklow,
> With forty stout men in his train,
> From the heart of the hills, where the spirit
> Of Freedom has dared to remain!

The Hanging of John Moore

The Reward

Drury said that he had seen a leaflet announcing "that it had been determined to offer a reward for the conviction of the murderer, and the names of the Wicklow gentry were appended, and the amount which each promised to subscribe. The list commenced with several sums of £50, then smaller amounts, and concluded with three contributions of £100 each." By comparison, rebel leader General Joseph Holt had only £300 on his head, and Michael Dwyer 500 guineas (£525). £1 then would be about €130 now.

The Hume Stone

Dickson (1944) said the site was marked with a granite boulder on the west side of the road between the Gap and Rathdangan. Martin Doyle of Rathdangan showed me the site of the "Hume Stone" on the boundary of Sleivereagh Upper and Ballyknockan a few hundred yards on the Rathdangan side of Ballinabarney Gap and said it had been removed in the 1970s. Local lore says that there was an indelible stain of blood on the stone.

---

[141] Campion, pp. 16-18.
[142] The modern name of the stone circle on Kilranelagh Hill and the townland to which it gives its name is Boleycarrigeen (locally pronounced "Ballycarrigeen") – "the summer pasture of the small stones".

The Vale of Avoca

Tigroney House

Not all authorities agree, but it is believed locally that "Tigroney", a townland name, derives from *Teach na Rómhánach* ("House of the Romans") and that this refers to Palladius, who was appointed bishop to the Irish Christians in 431, a year before Saint Patrick is said to have arrived. It is fairly certain that Palladius founded three churches in and near County Wicklow: at Avoca, Donard and Killeen Cormac near Dunlavin a half mile on the Kildare side of the border with Wicklow. Avoca people claim that church was his first.

Liam Price says the origin of Tigroney is more likely *Tigh Cróinín* ("House of Cronan").[143] Cronan was a prominent early medieval saint who is best known by the affectionate "Mochua", which name is retained in the nearby townland of Kilmacoo (Church of Mochua).

---

[143] Price, *Place-names*, p. 467.

Published Sources

Abbreviations

AFM – *Annals of the Four Masters* (in full: *Annals of the Kingdom of Ireland from the Earliest Times to the Year 1616*) – see O'Donovan, John.

DIL – *Dictionary of the Irish Language Based Mainly on Old and Middle Irish Materials*, Compact Edition, Royal Irish Academy, Dublin, 1983.

JKAS – *Journal of the Kildare Archaeological Society.*

JRSAI – *Journal of the Royal Society of Antiquaries of Ireland.*

RC – *Revue Celtique.*

Annals of Ireland, see O'Donovan, John, *Annals of Ireland.*

Arnott, Neil, *Elements of Physics*, Part I, 6th edition, Longman et al., London, 1864.

Avoca Local History Guide, see Irish Countrywomen's Association.

Bartlett, Thomas, "'Masters of the Mountains': The Insurgent Careers of Joseph Holt and Michael Dwyer, County Wicklow, 1798-1803", in Hannigan, op. cit.

Beatha Aodha Ruaidh Uí Dhomhnall, see Walsh, Paul.

Behan, Dominic, *Ireland Sings*, TRO Essex Music Ltd., 1973; Exclusive Distributors, Music Sales Corp/Ltd, New York, London.

Bernard, Bayle, *The Life of Samuel Lover*, King, London, 1874.

Brown, M. J., *Historical Ballad Poetry*, The Educational Company of Ireland, Dublin & Belfast, 1912.

Calendar of the Carew Manuscripts, J. S. Brewer and William Bullen, eds., Longmans et al., London, 1868.

Campion, John Thomas, MD, *Michael Dwyer or The Insurgent Captain of the Wicklow Mountains: A Tale of the Rising in '98*, Dublin; M.H. Gill & Son, Ltd, n.d. 1867?; Cameron, Ferguson & Co., Glasgow, n.d. 1867?. Campion was born in 1814 and died c. 1892.

Collins, Charles MacCarthy, *Irish Celtic Songs and Song-writers*, Cornish, London; Combridge, Dublin; 1885.

Cox, Richard, *Hibernia Anglicana or The History of Ireland from the Conquest Thereof to this Present Time*, Vol, 1, Joseph Watts, London, 1689.

Croker, T. Crofton, *Memoirs of Joseph Holt*, Vol. 1, Colburn, London, 1838.

Cullen, Luke, *Insurgent Wicklow 1798*, Ruan O'Donnell, ed., Kestrel Books, Bray, 1998; first published 1938.

Dickson, Charles, *The Life of Michael Dwyer*, Browne and Nolan Ltd., The Richview Press, Dublin, 1944.

Drury, C. M., "West County Wicklow Notes", JKAS 5, 1906-08.

Dublin Evening Post, 11 October 1798.

The Dublin Penny Journal.

Edwards, David, "In Tyrone's Shadow: Feagh McHugh, Forgotten Leader of the Nine Years War", in O'Brien, op. cit.

Falls, Cyril, *Elizabeth's Irish Wars*, Methuen & Co., London; Barnes & Noble, New York; 1950, 1970.

Faolain, Turlough, *Blood on the Harp: Irish Rebel History in Ballad*, Whitston, Troy, NY, 1983.

Glassie, Henry, ed., *Irish Folk Tales*, Pantheon, NYC, 1985.

Greene, David, *Fingal Rónáin and Other Stories*, School of Celtic Studies, Dublin Institute for Advanced Studies, Mediaeval and Modern Irish Series, Vol xvi; 1955.

Griffin, Gerald, *The Poetical Works of Gerald Griffin, Esq.*, London, Dublin & Edinburgh, 1843.

Griffin, Gerald, "Antrim Jack, and His General", in *Talis Qualis, or Tales of the Jury Room*, Duffy, Dublin & London, 1842.

Gwynn, Edward J., *The Metrical Dindshenchas*, Royal Irish Academy, Dublin, 1903-1935. Reprinted 1991 by the School of Celtic Studies, Dublin Institute for Advanced Studies.

Hale, Leslie, *John Philpot Curran: His Life and Times*, Cape, London, 1958.

Hannigan, Ken, and William Nolan, eds., *Wicklow History and Society: Interdisciplinary Essays on the History of an Irish County*, Geography Publications, Dublin, 1994.

Harding, David, and Randal Gray, *Weapons: An International Encyclopedia from 5000 BC to 2000 AD*, Diagram Visual Information, 1980, 1990.

Harding's Dublin Songster, Vol. 2, No. 15 (c.1850).

Hardiman, James, *Irish Minstrelsy or Bardic Remains of Ireland*, Vol. II, London, 1831; Irish University Press, Shannon, 1971.

Healy, James N., *The Second Book of Irish Ballads*, Mercier, 1962.

Irish Countrywomen's Association, local chapter, *Avoca Local History Guide*, written in 1974, updated and published in 1987. No page numbers.

The Irish Magazine, January 1810.

Joyce, P. W., *The Origin and History of Irish Names of Places*, Dublin, London, 1869.

Lawlor, Chris, "Dunlavin Green Revisited", in *Parish Link*, Vol. 4, No. 3, November 1998; an inter-parish newsletter covering Dunlavin, Donard and Davidstown.

Lawlor, Chris, *The Massacre on Dunlavin Green*, self-published: Chris Lawlor, Stephen Street, Dunlavin, Co. Wicklow, 1998.

Lewis, Samuel, *A Topographical Dictionary of Ireland*, 1837 (reissued 1970 by Kennikat Press, Port Washington, NY, and London).

Lockhart, J. G., *Memoirs of the Life of Sir Walter Scott, Bart.*, Cadell, Edinburgh, 1847.

Long, Harry, "Three Settlements of Gaelic Wicklow 1169-1600: Rathgall, Ballinacor and Glendalough", in Hannigan, op. cit.

Lover, Samuel, *Legends and Stories of Ireland*, Wakeman, Dublin; Baldwin and Cradock, London; Oliver and Boyd, Edinburgh, 1831.

Lover, Samuel, *Songs and Ballads*, Chapman & Hall, London, 1839; Bryce, London, 1858.

Mac Airt, Seán, *Leabhar Branach: The Book of the O'Byrnes*, The Dublin Institute for Advanced Studies, Dublin, 1944.

McCall, Patrick Joseph, *Songs of Erinn*, Simpton, Marshall, London; Gill, Dublin; 1899.

Mac Manus, Dermot, *The Middle Kingdom: The Faerie World of Ireland*, Colin Smythe, 1959, 1973.

Madden, R. R., *The Life and Times of Robert Emmet*, Haverty, New York, 1857.

Madden, R. R., ed., *Literary Remains of the United Irishmen of 1798*, Duffy, Dublin, 1887.

Madden, R. R., *The United Irishmen: Their Lives and Times*, Lea and Blanchard, Philadelphia, 1842.

Meyer, Kuno, *Hibernica Minora*, Oxford, 1894.

Moore, Thomas, *A Selection of Irish Melodies, with Symphonies and Accompaniments*, by Sir John Stevenson, Mus. Doc. and Characteristic words by Thomas Moore Esq., Powers, 1808.

Morgan, Hiram, *Tyrone's Rebellion*, Gill and Macmillan, Dublin, 1993.

Nicholls, K. W., "The Genealogy of the O'Byrnes of Ranelagh", in O'Brien, op. cit.

O'Brien, Conor, ed., *Feagh McHugh O'Byrne: The Wicklow Firebrand, A Volume of Quatercentennial Essays*, published as The Journal of the Rathdrum Historical Society, Volume I, 1998; Rathdrum Historical Society, c/o The Tourist Office, Rathdrum, Co. Wicklow.

O'Byrne (no first name), *Historical Reminiscences of O'Byrnes, O'Tooles, O'Kavanaghs and Other Irish Chieftains*, "printed for private circulation" by M'Gowan & Co., London, 1843.

O'Byrne, Emmet, "The Battle of Glenmalure, 25 August 1580 – Cause and Course", in O'Brien, op. cit.

Ó Dónaill, Niall, *Foclóir Gaeilge-Béarla*, Oifig an tSoláthair, Baile Átha Cliath, 1977.

O'Donnell, Ruan, "The Rebellion of 1798 in County Wicklow", in Hannigan, op. cit.

O'Donovan, John, ed/trans., *Annals of Ireland: Three Fragments copied from Ancient Sources by Dubhaltach Mac Firbisigh*, Irish Archaeological and Celtic Society, Dublin, 1860.

O'Donovan, John, trans., *Annals of the Kingdom of Ireland from the Earliest Times to the Year 1616*, (*Annals of the Four Masters*), Hodges & Smith, Dublin, 1856; De Búrca Rare Books, Dublin, 1990.

O'Farrell, Padraic, *Irish Ghost Stories*, Gill & Macmillan, Dublin, 2004.

O'Grady, Standish Hayes, *Silva Gadelica*, London & Edinburgh, 1892. [Standish Hayes O'Grady (1832-1915) and Standish James O'Grady (1846-1928) were cousins.]

O'Grady, Standish James, *The Flight of the Eagle*, Lawrence & Bullen, London, 1897; Talbot Press, Dublin, and Fisher Unwin, London, 1944; AMS Pr. Inc., New York, no date, in print 1996.

O'Grady, Standish James, *Red Hugh's Captivity: A Picture of Ireland, Social and Political, in the Reign of Queen Elizabeth*, Ward & Downey, London, 1889.

O'Kelly, E. P., "Historical Notes on Baltinglass", JKAS 5, 1906-08.

Ó hÓgáin, Dáithí, *Myth, Legend and Romance: An Encyclopaedia of the Irish Folk Tradition*, Prentice Hall Press, New York, and Ryan Publishing Company, UK, 1991.

O'Rahilly, T. F., "Buchet the Herdsman", *Ériu 16*, 1952.

O'Sullivan [var. O'Sullevan] Bear(e), Don Philip, *Ireland Under Elizabeth*, trans./ed., Matthew J. Byrne, SJ; Sealy, Bryers & Walker; Dublin, 1903; first published in Latin in Lisbon in 1621. Don Philip was born in Ireland c. 1592.

O'Sullivan, Patrick V., *Irish Superstitions and Legends of Animals and Birds*, Mercier, 1991.

O'Toole, Edward, "The Holy Wells of County Carlow", *Béaloideas* Vol 4, No. 2, 1933.

Ó Tuathail, Pádraig, ed., "Wicklow Traditions of 1798", *Béaloideas*, Vol 5, No. 2, Nollaig 1935.

Plummer, Charles, *Lives of Irish Saints*, Vol. II, Oxford, 1922.

Price, Liam, "Notes on Feagh Mc Hugh O'Byrne", JKAS 11, 1930.

Price, Liam, *The Place-names of Co. Wicklow*, Dublin Institute for Advanced Studies, Dublin, 1946, 1983.

Russell, Micho, *Micho's Dozen: Traditional Songs from the Repertoire of Micho Russell*, Ennistymon Festival of Traditional Singing, (no date, c. 1991).

Shearman, John Francis, *Loca Patriciana, an Identification of Localities, Chiefly in Leinster, Visited by Saint Patrick ...*, M. H. Gill & Sons, Dublin, 1879.

Spenser, Edmund, *A View of the Present State of Ireland*, W. L. Renwick, ed., Oxford: Clarendon Press, 1970.

Stokes, Whitley, "The Rennes Dindshenchas", RC 15, 1894.

Sullivan, Timothy Daniel, *A Selection from the Songs and Poems of T. D. Sullivan*, Sealy, Bryers and Walker; Gill; Dublin, 1899.

Thackeray, William Makepeace, *The Irish Sketch-book by Mr. M. A. Titmarsh*, Vol II, Chapman and Hall, London, 1843.

Vose, John D., *Tales and Yarns of Glendalough and the Wicklow Hills*, told to John D. Vose by Bill Fanning, Shepherd of Glendalough, published by J. D. Vose, 24 Norcliffe Rd., Blackpool, FY2 9AW. No date; c. 1995.

Walsh, Paul, trans. and ed., *Beatha Aodha Ruaidh Uí Dhomhnall*, by Lughaidh Ó Clérigh, Vol 1 (text and translation), Irish Texts Society, Dublin, 1948.

Walshe, Patrick T., "The Antiquities of the Dunlavin-Donard District", JRSAI 61, 1931.
Wicklow Commemorating 1798-1998, Calendar of Events, Wicklow County Council, 1997.

Oral Sources

Jim Byrne, Jr, of Rathdangan
Martin Doyle of Rathdangan
Gladys of Graigue
Mrs Whittle of Donard
Patrick Clark of Avoca
Betty Bolger of Avoca
Jimmy Doyle and his son James of Avoca
Mick Howlett of Avoca
Jimmy Treacy of Avoca
Dara Clear of Rathdrum
Caroline Moules of Aughrim
Aiden Seerick of County Mayo
Mattie Lennon of Lacken
John Glennon of Hollywood

About the Author

Richard Marsh, storyteller and Legendary Tour guide, lived in the Vale of Avoca during the 1980s. Now a Dublin resident, he visits Irish schools with the Heritage in Schools and the Writers in Schools schemes to tell stories of Ireland, Spain, the Basque Country, and many world cultures.

His Legendary Tours take people to the places in Ireland where the myths and legends happened, and he tells the stories on location. For those who can't come to Ireland, he brings the stories regularly to other countries on his storytelling tours.

RTÉ Radio One listeners will be familiar with Richard's voice on such programmes as Sunday Miscellany and Just A Thought / Matins / The Living Word.

Forthcoming in the Legendary Books Series:

Medieval Irish Legends
Spanish and Basque Legends
Galician Legends and Tales

Author photo by Isabel Severing